Education and Community

Related titles

Philosophy of Education – Richard Pring
Analysing Underachievement in Schools – Emma Smith
Theory of Education – David Turner
Private Education – Geoffrey Walford
Markets and Equity in Education – Geoffrey Walford

EDUCATION AND COMMUNITY

Dianne Gereluk

continuum
LONDON • NEW YORK

KH

Continuum International Publishing Group

The Tower Building   15 East 26th Street
11 York Road   New York
London SE1 7NX   NY 10010

www.continuumbooks.com

© Dianne Gereluk 2006

British Library Cataloguing-in-Publication Data
A catalogue record for this book is available from the British Library.

ISBN 0–8264–8466–2 (hardback)

Library of Congress Cataloging-in-Publication Data
A catalog record for this book is available from the Library of Congress.

Typeset by YHT Ltd, London
Printed and bound in Great Britain by Antony Rowe Ltd, Chippenham, Wiltshire

3/16/07

To my daughter, Katya

May you feel part of a community that both cherishes your individual spirit and develops the social bonds that enhance our lives as humans.

Acknowledgements

This work, in many respects, is a manifestation of community. Many people have been an integral part of my community, and my heartfelt appreciation and warmth for them have made the culmination of this research possible.

It has been a privilege to work under the mentorship of Harry Brighouse and David Halpin. This community of three has provided a solid backbone to my research. I have grown from this symbiotic relationship, learning and building upon our strengths. The philosophical perspective of Harry Brighouse complemented the socio-theoretical and pedagogic perspectives of David Halpin, both weaving effortlessly between the disciplines, and offering advice in all aspects of my research. It was a pure joy to be a part of these conversations.

To my parents, no words can describe the love and gratitude that I feel for both of you. You have taught me much over the years where books do not do justice: tenacity, kindness and courage are but a few that come to mind. I am proud to be your daughter.

Finally, to my husband Marlow, who has had to endure every bump during this journey, sharing in my successes and lifting my spirits during my trials and tribulations. Your unwavering support and encouragement helped me more than you probably know.

Contents

Introduction

The promotion of community is widely thought to be an important educational aim, benefiting individuals and society as a whole. However, the precise nature of community is far from clear. If it is difficult to articulate distinctive features of communities, then it is necessarily difficult to specify clear objectives to guide educators in the promotion of communities in schools.

Such lack of clarity is demonstrated by the divergent use of 'community' in education policy documents, aims and objectives, curricular frameworks and discussions of pedagogy. The imprecise nature of community supports a need for a broader theoretical discussion about the nature and importance of communities. This has significant implications for how educators are to conceptualize and promote community.

Further, local and global civil changes have implications for how individuals see their place in society, and concomitant repercussions for how people relate to political, cultural and social communities.

Given such change, schools are increasingly called upon to provide opportunities for children to flourish in communal relationships, thus increasing future prospects to pursue the goods which community provides. This presents educators with new challenges and opportunities. How are communities created and fostered in schools? Do any types of communities suffice to fulfil a school's obligation to foster them? Are some communities worth constraining, and are others beneficial? It is one thing to become involved in communities on a daily basis; it is another to consider how schools ought to play a role in fostering communities. The ambiguous directive to promote community in schools gives rise to asking what it is that is important about community, and how best that may be fostered.

In order to develop a conception of community that is relevant for education policy and practice, it is necessary first to step back from the non-ideal realities of school life, and consider the concept of community at a high level of abstraction. An important aspect of this book will be to develop principles that evaluate which communities we find valuable and worthwhile in a liberal society. Once theoretical principles are developed, we can then bridge this theoretical discussion with contemporary schooling conditions. As such, three distinct parts weave between the theoretical and educational discussions about community.

This book has three aims. The first is to articulate and discern various characteristics of communities. The second is to develop a philosophical conception of community drawing primarily from Rawls' liberal theory and, subsequently, to show how the corresponding normative principles are applicable to schooling. The third aim is to consider the changing nature of communities in the light of contemporary social conditions in schools and society. In drawing these three strands together, an evaluative framework emerges that can help guide educators in the task of discerning and promoting particular types of communities in education policy and practice. The book, accordingly, is divided into three parts to address each of these aims.

Part I sets the argument for why there is a need to provide normative principles to help guide educators' conceptions of community in education. Chapter 1 begins with my personal narrative to illustrate my interest in and difficulty with communities. These experiences have called into question what it means to promote community, and how a normative theory may help clarify the types of community we wish to promote in education. Chapter 2 positions this debate by locating various uses of community in educational contexts. The objective of Chapter 2 highlights multiple and competing visions of community in education policy and school documents, noting ambiguities and conflicting aims as they arise. Chapter 3 sets out the problematic aspects of community in relation to individual rights. Specifically it looks at three tensions in the promotion of community: internal community practices that infringe the basic liberties of its individual members; exclusive membership in a community; and dominant community practices that infringe basic liberties of individuals external to the community. Chapter 4 considers common characteristics that people consider to be valuable in community. It articulates communitarian perspectives, and also highlights potential goods that we may derive from community.

Part II builds upon the characteristics of community, both good and bad, and develops a normative theory. Chapter 5 develops a liberal conception of community, and provides procedural principles that provide the basis for conduct for communities within the boundaries of reasonable pluralism. Chapter 6 considers three case studies to illustrate how liberal principles may evaluate the permissibility of certain communities for schooling. Chapter 7 concludes by applying normative liberal principles for the promotion of particular communities in schools.

Part III re-envisions community education in the light of these normative principles within the social realities of schools and society. Chapter 8 looks at the changing social dynamic of society and its implications for promoting community. Chapter 9 examines the internal challenges and obstacles for fostering community in schools. Chapter 10 ends with a summary of how liberal principles can inform a particular conception of community, and some exploratory suggestions that may create a more conducive environment for fostering liberal communities.

CHAPTER 1

The Promise and Paradox of Community

Notions of 'community' are found in almost every educational context. Schools, for example, are enjoined to foster it among their staff and students and to encourage it within the areas they serve. Similar tendencies are reflected in higher educational institutions. In neither case are these tendencies restricted to one part of the world or one specific period in time. Yet, it is noticeable that the prevalence of discussions about community within education has been rejuvenated in recent times: some attribute the re-emphasis on community as a consequence of and response to global market influences and changes in civil society. In both instances, there is a perceived and real diminished sense of being a part of community. Much of the burden has been placed on schools to rekindle community both formally and informally through education policies and practices, benefiting students and society.

Whether community is prevalent in educational discussions does not appear to be at issue: there is an abundance of literature about promoting it in schools and creating closer links between schools and community. It is issues that do not appear to be addressed in contemporary literature, or those that should be addressed, which I will consider. Before we can implement policy reforms that encourage stronger community initiatives, it is fruitful to have a theoretical discussion as to what aspects, in particular, we find important about community. Theoretical principles can then assist educators in fostering particular types of community that are considered valuable.

There may be initial bemusement with the need for having such a discussion. Some may simply assume that promoting community in schools is beneficial: 'Isn't community just a part of education. What is there to say about it?' Others may ask, 'Hasn't this question been discussed before?' Still others may simply reject the question on the basis that it is mere 'academic play'. They may challenge the validity of such a question by commenting, 'What relevance does thinking about community have for policy-makers and educators in the real world?'

Community has affected each of us in some way, whether or not we are conscious of it. Some have benefited from being part of a positive community environment. Others have had negative experiences of being excluded from or being marginalized in a community. Probably most people have experienced both. To illustrate this, I begin with my experience, not because it is necessarily unique or pivotal to the nature of this research, but to illustrate how personal problems elicit public concerns (Mills 1970: 18).[1]

Three major influences were instrumental in generating my interest and the impetus for conducting research about notions of 'community'. The first was my upbringing and participation in a left-wing Ukrainian association in Canada. The second was my experiences as a Ukrainian bilingual primary teacher in a trilingual-track school. The third was my earlier research on the notion of 'choice' in Alberta charter schools. I shall describe how each of these experiences contributed to my thinking and perplexity about communities.

Life in an ethnic community

The Association of United Ukrainian Canadians (AUUC) was first established in 1918 in Winnipeg, Canada. The stated primary aims of the AUUC were to provide and foster an appreciation of Ukrainian culture within the Canadian multicultural society. The organization had a politically progressive platform, advocating workers' rights, health care and peace. At the height of the association, it had grown to 185 branches, including women's and youth branches. Two newspapers (*Ukrainian Labour News* and *Farmer's Life*) and two magazines (*Working Woman* and *Youth World*) were being published on a regular basis. The organization had a widespread network of children's schools, as well as adult education classes.

My involvement in the Association of United Ukrainian Canadians started at the age of three at the local Ukrainian cultural centre in Edmonton. My participation over the years within the organization evolved slowly from mere local cultural activities to a more political role. The organization offered song, music and dance for children and adults, held summer children's camps, youth workshops and seminars, and had leadership development courses for later political participation in the organization. My involvement slowly spanned all areas of the organization. At the height of my participation I concurrently was a dance director and orchestra conductor, held positions on the local council and the national executive board, was an artistic director for a national festival and was a national coordinator for the development of a cultural cadre across Canada. Much of my identity was largely influenced by my participation within this Ukrainian organization. It is also where I developed a strong community activism that continued in other endeavours in my life. While on the national executive board of the AUUC, I became increasingly conscious of the complexity involved in fostering this cultural and political community.

Similar to other non-profit organizations that have lost prominence (Putnam 2000), the AUUC faced many challenges. Prominent among these were membership decline, diminished participation of younger members and a lack of a clear mandate in the light of contemporary changes and social climate. Many factors seemed to hamper the evolution of this community. While structural changes had occurred a decade before, changing from a model based on the former Soviet political structure to a more contemporary organizational structure, resistance to change former habits often hampered the implementation of these changes. Further, while explicit statements were made at the national level to encourage new members to participate in the various levels of the organization, many of the older members felt threatened and suspicious of newer members who, they felt, did not possess the values of the organization's founders. These factors, increasingly, led members to become embittered in internal power struggles and infighting. Due to these tensions, membership loss was exacerbated and enticement of new participants to join became increasingly difficult. Similarly, older members became disenchanted by the present deterioration and breakdown of the organization that they had built up during their youth. The intergenerational struggle was prevalent between old and young. New challenges such as increasingly mixed-ethnic families, altering the cultural demographics, created new complexities. Finally, external political changes and social movements that the organization had once rallied around had changed, causing an increasing loss of vision or purpose.

Both my positive and negative experiences with the AUUC have brought a heightened awareness of the complexity of community: the potential benefits in having a sense of belonging, and the exclusivity and traditionalism that can make change difficult. External societal changes and internal membership dynamics made transitions difficult to sustain and traditions difficult to change in this community.

From ethnic community to bilingual primary teacher

My teaching experience began as a primary bilingual teacher in a public school system in Canada. I taught in a trilingual track school where Ukrainian, French and English programmes were offered. Between the three language programmes inequities of funding, resources and social capital were noticeable. My observations and experiences of teaching in a trilingual school influenced my ways of thinking about community and its implications for schooling.

The majority of my teaching assignment was devoted to teaching Ukrainian bilingual students. In this grouping of students, parents were 'active-choosers'.[2] Almost exclusively, children had one or both parents who were of Ukrainian heritage or were Ukrainian immigrants. Students did not come from the local vicinity, but spanned many areas of the city. Although students were bused in, parents were a physical and vocal presence. Much of the parent council comprised parents from the Ukrainian programme. Parents often knew each other from their involvement in Ukrainian Catholic and Orthodox organizations as well as other, secular community and cultural organizations. They organized fundraising events, mainly through bingo and casinos, and gave tremendous financial and human resources specifically to the Ukrainian classes.[3] As such, the Ukrainian parents were a strong 'lobby group' and a dominant force in the school.

Parents whose children were enrolled in the French immersion programme did not have the same status. Some indicators seem to suggest why there was a difference between the French and Ukrainian programmes. Students in the French immersion programme were a more heterogeneous group. Parents still tended to be active-choosers, but not to the same extent as the Ukrainian parents. Many parents enrolled their children in the French language programme to give their children the opportunity of learning a second language, but not necessarily to promote a particular heritage. Parents were not necessarily of French heritage nor were they French immigrants, unlike the Ukrainian programme. While they were interested in the development of their children, they were not as organized as the parents from the Ukrainian programme. They did not generate as much fundraising, although they would help in other ways such as volunteering for the school.

The final grouping of students was the English track students. They tended to come from the local vicinity, rather than being largely bused in from the other areas like the Ukrainian and French-programme students. Students enrolled in this programme often fell into three categories: parents who did not value learning a second language; parents who felt that it would be more beneficial for their children to focus solely on the core subjects without expending time toward learning a second language, or students who were discouraged from taking a second language due to a perceived learning or behaviour difficulty that might impede learning two languages. They were often considered impoverished, either as a result of parents who did not wish to put their children in a second-language programme or who could not because they were academically weak. Parents of these students tended to be a more invisible group, sporadically involved in the activities of the school.

There were thus significantly inequitable educational programmes at this school. The Ukrainian parents had the most 'social capital',[4] and often became a dominant grouping of the school. Teachers often felt that many of the parents in the Ukrainian programme were 'aggressive parents' (Kohn 1998), putting demands on the school for the specific advantage of their child. They had a strong homogeneous grouping of parents who were able to mobilize and capitalize on the strengths of their established external Ukrainian community to continue to lobby and create a stronger overpowering voice than the other two language programmes. This was to the advantage of Ukrainian students who benefited from their parents' extensive advocacy, but it did so to the disadvantage of students in the other two language programmes who did not have the same level of involvement from their parents. Within the competing language communities in schools, Ukrainian students appeared to have a distinct positional advantage over the other two language programmes, receiving more educational resources, having smaller class sizes and attaining consistently higher educational achievement scores.

A return to theory

My unease with the positional advantage attained by Ukrainian students led me to examine Alberta charter schools (Gereluk 1998). If the effects of parental influence were noticeable in a public school setting, I wondered what further implications parental choice would have in allowing parents increased educational choice and influence in charter schools. I also wondered whether this would result in increased educational inequities in public education.

Charter schools are intended to provide alternative educational programmes not currently offered in the public school setting. They develop a specific educational mandate, focusing on a particular pedagogical practice, specialized curricula or specific student needs. Schools hope to attract students (and parents) who share the same educational mandate that the charter school has set. Charter schools are given more flexibility and latitude from governmental regulations and governing practices. In turn, charter schools are expected to demonstrate three things: the school is financially viable; the school has fulfilled its mandate; and students demonstrate greater academic achievement.

It could be said that these charter schools exhibit particular types of communities, creating schools based on shared educational ideals and aims. This was reflected in interviews, where it was felt that there was a greater sense of community. Charter school administrators and governing board members attributed much of this to smaller class sizes, smaller school population, sustained and ongoing relations among staff and parents, and a clear and shared educational mandate.

Charter schools also used informal selection criteria to attract certain students to their charter school who would match the school community. Various practices were used such as marketing their school to specific student populations, having interviews and entrance requirements, and requiring parental and student contracts that set out specific responsibilities and obligations. Charter school administrators and board members justified these practices on the basis that they wanted to match the school with the student's needs and, in turn, that the student would commit to the educational ideals of the school.

Educational researchers note their uneasiness with these forms of selectivity in order to create a more unified school community (Kenway 1993; Wringe 1994; Fuller and Elmore 1996; Whitty 1997a). The concern is that such selection practices and specialist schools will disadvantage and exclude particular students, especially those that may be perceived as being more difficult or expensive to teach. Despite the rationale for creating stronger school communities, such reforms may have the unintended consequence of compromising issues of social justice and equity.

Examining charter schools heightened my awareness of the complexities surrounding the issue of community. In certain respects, I could identify with some of the strategies used to foster a stronger sense of community. In other ways, I was uneasy with the potential for charter schools to exclude 'undesirable' students and create exclusive school communities. The notion of community was becoming increasingly a double-edged sword both for what it potentially promoted and concealed.

If my unease with community was palpable from my own personal and professional experiences, how was it that community could so easily be endorsed in schools and education more generally? How could I reconcile the benefits that I clearly valued from some of my associations with various communities with the potential repercussions of exclusivity and marginalization?

These narratives highlight my personal difficulties with community, but more importantly, draw attention to tensions that are apparent in fostering community in education policy and practice.

Concepts of 'community'

Promoting community in schools is generally taken for granted: it is important for schools to foster community. Yet, what does it mean to promote 'community'? A school can foster community in innumerable ways. Its intrigue captivates our gaze and causes bewilderment. In the light of the magnitude of the task, a simple definition of community seems like an appropriate place to begin.

The root term of community is derived from the Latin word *communis*, having etymological links to *with obligation* and *together* (Williams 1979). Historical developments on the notion of community invoke elements of the 'common concern' or the 'common organization' (Williams 1983: 76). Further, community rarely or never has connotations of negativity, nor has 'positive opposing' terms (ibid.: 76). Plant (1974) suggests that there is a descriptive and evaluative element to community. Descriptively, community can be linked to a 'locality, to identity of functional interests, to a sense of belonging, to shared cultural and ethnic ideas and values, to a way of life opposed to the organisation and bureaucracy of modern mass society' (p. 13). There is a normative implication of what community should be, considering the collective values that are worth sustaining in society (ibid.: 13–15).

A definition is a logical place to start, yet this does not seem to be adequate: community in this context is still nebulous. For individuals, belonging to a community arguably has numerous positive benefits associated with having a sense of belonging and commitment. Similarly, it is hoped that community will provide stability for society, bringing individuals together through shared values and common aims within private and public spheres. Conversely, discrepancies are found between ideal versions of community, and the non-ideal circumstances in actual communities: power differentials, traditionalism, and oppressive practices do not feature in this definition.

Various literatures on citizenship refer to community as a pivotal aspect within civic republicanism and democratic theories (Gutmann 1987, Phillips 1993, McKnight 1995, Barber 1998). Their literatures address notions of community through aspects of political participation and decentralized local control. These theories contend that individuals need to be empowered by voice and opportunities for participation. It is not enough for individuals to live in a society based solely on rights and responsibilities; rather, society needs to be held together by something more than that – by community and fraternity (Oldfield 1998). While this body of literature reveals the ties of belonging to community and political participation through grassroots community movements, it is less able to reconcile internal constraints of membership often found within communities.

Contemporary communitarians criticize the diminished sense of community and the corresponding need for its restoration. Communitarians vary in their perspectives. Philosophical communitarians tend to emphasize the nature of the self in relation to the community. Some communitarians assert that individuals are born into a particular community, and in this way, are 'encumbered selves' (Sandel 1998). We cannot separate the self from one's community: we are born into particular families, practices and traditions. Starting from this ontological premise, the communities into which we are born are key to developing accepted virtues (MacIntyre 1981). Communities have established social practices and traditions that have been passed down from generation to generation – collective values which individuals naturally imbue through their communities. Communities are constitutive of the self and, as such, are to be embraced and accepted as a necessary condition of human life. For philosophical communitarians, community is a unitary construction, already present from birth, and essential to human development. Dismissal of community is neither possible nor desirable from a communitarian perspective. Being born into a community is a prima facie fact, unalterable, except within the confines of that community. This is a strong conception of community, and one that is difficult to accept for two reasons: first, individuals are unable to leave or dismiss their constitutive communities; second, community is both unitary and singular, with little consideration for one's participation in multiple communities (I will discuss this in more depth in Chapter 4).

Political communitarians advocate a recommitment to community values: society, in their view, has developed a culture whereby individuals believe they have rights with little corresponding responsibilities. Etzioni (1993) suggests that this has led to excessive individualism and a decline of the common good. Political communitarians believe that community will help in rebuilding a sense of commitment and obligation to people. Further, community can help to achieve a common good through attaining consensus via deliberations in community.

Despite the positive overtures for a rejuvenation of community life, implicit conservative undertones are apparent throughout the literature. First, there is a troubling emphasis on consensus and deliberation at the local community. Communitarians seem rather unconcerned with those in the minority, and contend that the voice of the majority is appropriate for developing community values. Second, communitarian theory requires that citizens reconnect to the moral values that enhance the social fabric of society. For political communitarians, this entails: a commitment to strong family values – preferably two-parent families with an emphasis on the child; a development of moral foundations and character development in schools; and a recommitment to the common moral values found in the local community. This new secular spin of communitarianism put forth and popularized by Etzioni (1993) and others (Bell 1993, Tam 1998) bases much hope on tradition and accepted norms and behaviours as the pillars of a stable civil society. Political communitarians celebrate the promise of community in rebuilding society, yet fail to recognize the problematic aspects inherent in using consensus as a way in which to determine common goods for society.

Feminist perspectives on community tend to address two main themes. The first prominent theme addresses the internal dynamics of community, particularly concerning substantive inequalities in communities. Notions of exclusivity, lack of voice, minority rights and the positioning of individuals are prominent themes in these readings (Fraser 1999, Okin 1999, Knight-Abowitz 2000, Fendler 2001). The second dominant theme considers the instrumental value that communities can possess by having a collective voice for political action (Fraser and Lacey 1993, Phillips 1995, Mouffe 2000, Young 2000). Though recognizing power differentials in communities, having representation through a collective voice may be a more effective way to change substantive inequalities in society, rather than by individual representation. The focus in both strands of feminist readings relies on dominant discourses of power in communities. The former is a critique of internal mechanisms that marginalize and suppress individual interests through community dynamics. The latter considers the potential to alter the substantive inequalities of society through collective action.

The strength of this position rests in articulating the problematic aspects of community. However, the prescriptive solutions rest heavily with political processes of protecting minority representation and voice. It does not consider, however, whether attaining representation is sufficient in and of itself to change perceived oppressive practices in communities. A great reliance rests on political representation and political process, with little attention to theoretical principles that may assist in changing unacceptable internal practices of communities.

Social theorists have also taken great interest in societal trends and their effect on communities. There has been a pervasive concern about the declining nature of community, which is not a new phenomenon. Tönnies (1957) warned citizens of the declining nature of *Gemeinschaft*-like communities: communities based on kinship and friendship. Changes to civil society had seen a proliferation of *Gesellschaft* communties: associations based on economic necessity and individual advantage. Tocqueville (1956) similarly observed the newly formed democracy of the United States in the late 1700s. In individuals' pursuit of equality and liberty, Tocqueville felt that people had dismissed the third key

pillar – that of fraternity. The thoughts of Tönnies and Tocqueville, however, still persist in contemporary discussions. Putnam's
research (2000) considers declining membership trends in formal
not for profit organizations in the United States.

A radical departure from Tönnies' critique of the diminishing
Gemeinschaft communities was that of Marx and Rousseau, who
both saw the pivotal changes in the workplace as formed through
industrial cooperation as central to their idea of community (Plant
1974: 25). Fraternity and cooperation were the pivotal features of
these idyllic communities, challenging the hierarchical and conservative nature of rural communities, recommending one that
was based on a shared awareness of humanity.

Classical sociologists may heed warnings of a decline of community in society. However, the work of Beck (1999) and Giddens (1998) suggest that communities are always in flux in
keeping with the changing needs of society. As certain communities diminish in import, others rise in their place. The germi-
nation of new types of communities reflects this social
phenomenon. Communities do not become defunct, but are fluid
and temporary. The sociological perspective offers indicators for
concern, but also suggests new possibilities for change.

The final step, which I wish to develop further to provide
principles that will discern between better and worse communities, is an analysis of liberal political philosophy. I argue that
liberal theory can suggest a particular conception of community
that is desirable to espouse and apply in schooling. I will primarily
use Rawls (1971: 2000) to show how egalitarian liberalism can
offer better alternatives in which to uphold liberties of individuals
without necessarily compromising the collective aspects of community. In doing this, I want to suggest that liberal theories do
promote notions of community. They also offer a conception of
community which has a more flexible relationship between
individual and community than communitarian theories. Finally,
liberal theory articulates normative principles that can assist educators in distinguishing between positive and negative types of
community.

On the school treadmill: what do we need to be doing now?!
Educational reform often emphasizes the practical 'doing' of
community, through a patchwork of disjointed projects and
policy statements. Fay (1975) describes this as a policy science
approach in which the preoccupation is on concrete

implementation, action oriented and apparently value-free assumptions. Policies are continually developed, with seemingly little reflection of wider society. This has been the case in terms of implementing community practices in education. Teachers are often overwhelmed with the insurmountable policies issued from 'above', deciding which ones to honour and which ones to disregard (Hargreaves 1994). In addition to increased accountability and technocratic measures of the National Curriculum and Ofsted, it is not surprising that cross-curricular objectives such as community get pushed to one side, giving priority to core subjects rather than abstract and nebulous aims (Whitty, Rowe and Aggleton 1994). Community is everywhere, yet it is nowhere. By that, I suggest that community is placed in policy and school documents in various ways, never fully explored or expanded, only to be left dangling on the educational periphery. Successful examples of school communities emerge that we can all point to, but whether they can be found on a large scale is more difficult.

Pring (2000) speculates that much of the criticism of educational research is a result of researchers having little or no recognition of their theoretical and philosophical positions (pp. 5–7). Similar to Fay's (1975) criticisms of the over-emphasis on implementation, he argues that researchers need to examine the philosophical underpinnings in order to understand the 'nature of that which is to be researched into' (p. 6). A lack of theoretical understanding may have unintended consequences for researchers who may stride forth in their work, not examining the premises upon which their research rests. This resonates with my unease and my subsequent impetus for pursuing a theoretical analysis about community in relation to school practice and policy. By considering community at an abstract theoretical level, we can clarify some of the disputes and distinguish between the relevant issues that remain convoluted and complex in non-ideal circumstances, and provide prescriptive principles that assist in our evaluation of communities for school policy and practice.

Up until this point, I have taken as a given that it is an important aim to promote communities in schools; yet I have not provided a compelling answer that suggests the reasons why schools should promote communities. Such reasons require further theoretical discussion. Chapters 3 and 4 provide an articulation of the main issues that surround this debate, articulating negative and positive aspects of community in relation to education.

Before I branch out into a broader theoretical analysis of community, I first wish to survey the various ways community has been discussed in education policy and school documents. The consequences of having an ambiguous notion of 'community' are played out in the multiple, and sometimes contradictory, ways that it is conceived and implemented in school policy and practice.

We can talk about encouraging and fostering communities in schools in a general manner with relative ease, but once we try to be precise about what that involves, what it is that is important and how best that may be achieved, agreement is likely to disappear. By highlighting the ambiguous and problematic aspects of community in school policy and practice, Chapter 2 provides sufficient justification for why there is a need for a broader theoretical discussion about community.

Notes

1. I have borrowed this approach from Cohen (2000) who shows how his personal story of growing up in a Jewish community in Montreal fits into the larger philosophical question of egalitarianism. Telling my story highlights the complexities and tensions in participating in community, which in turn helps to locate the philosophical questions.

2. The term 'active-choosers' has become a common phrase used in the choice movement literature. Parents who are active-choosers tend to seek out an educational programme that meets their child's perceived individual needs. They may also look to alternative educational programmes that are not necessarily offered in their local catchment area.

3. For example, the parents' group would purchase computers for each of the Ukrainian classrooms, books would be bought for the specific classes, and field trips would be subsidized for Ukrainian students.

4. Social capital can be described as the amount of resources (cultural, social and economic) that enable a person to have greater ability to negotiate their positional value. For example, a person who has better education, greater network ties, more financial resources, etc., will have an easier time securing more positive social relationships and advantages than someone who has less of these types of resources (Bourdieu 1986).

PART I

Community and Education

CHAPTER 2

Community Directives for Schooling

References to community in education policy and school documents are marked. This phenomenon is not specific to a particular country or a particular time. Community is a recurring aim in education that captivates and bewilders educators. Its enigmatic nature, for the most part, goes without much notice: educators attempt to promote community in various ways. This ad hoc process inevitably creates numerous ways in which to envisage and practise community: this can foster creativity and potential and, conversely, allow the emergence of detrimental communities.

I begin by looking at the aims and objectives of the National Curriculum of England (DfEE 1999) to illustrate the general ambiguity regarding community. Other countries have similar references to community in general aims and objectives, civic education, multiculturalism and social justice (Western and Northern Canadian Protocol 2000, US Department of Education 2001, for instance). I draw on the National Curriculum of England to demonstrate this emphasis on community. I then consider five areas that point to various community directives for schooling. The first considers greater links between schools and other communities. The second focuses on community schools. The third area examines schools founded on communities of interest. The fourth area focuses on community directives in the curricular subject areas. The last considers informal practices and norms that are suggestive of fostering community.

Aims and objectives
References about community are cited, either explicitly or implicitly, four times in the aims and objectives of the National

Curriculum (DfEE 1999). If the aims and objectives are to be reflected in the practices of schools, then schools must consider how to foster community. I consider the ways in which the aims and objectives provide multiple directives in the promotion of communities for schooling.

The first aim provides a rationale for the value of relationships and why education should foster them:

> Education should reflect the enduring values that contribute to these ends. These include valuing ourselves, our families and other relationships, the wider groups to which we belong, the diversity in our society and the environment in which we live. (ibid.: 10)

The premise is that it is valuable for individuals to form various relationships, reflecting pluralist society. I wish to address two aspects in this statement: relationships are valuable for a person's well-being; and diverse relationships, reflecting a plurality of interests and backgrounds, are good for society. This statement assumes that the promotion of community is in the best interests of individuals and society, and that certain values should be encouraged that will promote this communal disposition. It does not address the types of community that would imbue these values considered to be important in developing such relationships.

The second aim of community addresses students' abilities to form relationships in the community:

> The school curriculum should promote students' self-esteem and emotional well-being and help them to form and maintain worthwhile and satisfying relationships, based on respect for themselves and for others, at home, school, work and in the community. It should develop their ability to relate to others and work *for the common good* [emphasis added]. (ibid.: 11)

This runs in a similar vein, but with a particular emphasis on a child's ability to form relationships beyond the confines of the school towards work and community outside school. Here, community refers to a geographically based location. It is difficult to denote whether 'in the community' refers to the local vicinity, or whether this implies some larger abstract notion of larger society. Perhaps it refers to both, but it is not clear at this point. If schools are to reflect and foster students' relationships to the external community, then it may be important to understand the extent of this aim.

This statement also suggests that students work with others 'for the common good'. The common good, however, is left unconsidered and undefined. A notion of the common good is controversial among liberals and feminists, for its teleological nature, and its tendency for dominant authoritative practices to suppress those in the minority or who are marginalized (Okin 1999, Young 2000, Nussbaum 2003). This question will be considered in more depth in Chapter 3. Considering what the common good entails has significant consequences for how community is to be addressed by schools.

The second aim also has the beginnings of a normative principle in that the formation of such relationships must be both 'worthwhile' and 'satisfying', and that it is based on 'respect for themselves and for others'. Therefore, communities that we may wish to promote in schools are to be compatible with respecting oneself and others, and that are worthwhile and satisfying. The first condition of respect for oneself and others appears to be self-explanatory. It is less clear as to what constitutes a worthwhile and satisfying relationship, and who decides what makes it 'worthwhile' or 'satisfying'.

A student might consider a worthwhile relationship to be one that increases her social status among her peers. Consequently, she may have a perceived sense of increased self-esteem and emotional well-being due to this relationship. However, the group may, for example, persuade her to shoplift, be truant or perform other unacceptable acts of behaviour that may be detrimental to her and to a wider community. In such a case, it might be useful for schools to distinguish and perhaps model various worthwhile relationships, and consider certain constraints schools may wish to adopt to help students negotiate their participation in various relationships.

Further, it is not clear who decides what makes a worthwhile relationship. One view is to think that relationships are only worthwhile and satisfying if they are beneficial to the individuals who are involved in the particular relationship, and more importantly, that each individual finds the relationship worthwhile. Others might add that there is value in creating worthwhile and satisfying relationships, which may have greater benefit than merely considering the private interests of each individual. What constitutes a worthwhile and satisfying relationship, and who decides if a relationship is worthwhile and whether it should be pursued, are matters that are left unexamined.

The third aim of community is cited as a form of participation. The concept of community in this sense is an active process or engagement, coupled with a notion of autonomy. It states:

> It should prepare students for the next steps in their education, training and employment and equip them to make informed choices at school and throughout their lives, enabling them to appreciate the relevance of their achievements to life and society outside school, including leisure, community engagement and employment. (ibid.: 12)

The emphasis here is on preparing students to have the capacity to understand and act upon various life choices, including engagement in community affairs. It assumes that students are (and perhaps should be) engaged in the affairs of the community and, in order to do so, require the ability to make informed judgements about how best to do that. The tenor of this statement is focused on both personal autonomy and a civic component about engaging in the public sphere.

The final reference to community is in its conclusion. Schools are to transmit the above aims as a matter of local and national priority, reflecting the ethos of their local community:

> This framework is designed to enable all schools to respond effectively to national and local priorities, to meet the individual learning needs of all students and to develop a distinctive character and ethos rooted in their local communities. (ibid.: 12)

Here, the reference to community can be interpreted as either a location or a set of common values or aims (or perhaps both): schools will reflect and respect the values of the external community by fostering similar values within the school environment. This is problematic for a number of reasons.

First, it assumes that there is one definitive, or homogeneous, character of a local community. Second, this position assumes few or no conflicting aims and values in communities or between communities. In such cases, it may be difficult for schools to recognize the ethos of a particular community. The statement assumes that schools will not have to contend with competing values and aims in and between communities, which they may have difficulty in resolving.

Similarly, the statement does not consider that students may not come from the local proximity of the school, but span many different areas beyond the local catchment area. Again, while the local community of the school may reflect similar traits and characteristics, some students may come from vastly different communities from the one in which the school is located.

Finally, and perhaps most importantly, it assumes that the values of the local community may be the types of values that we wish to promote in schools. While in healthy, vibrant communities this may be the case; in other situations, we may want to resist and challenge the values of the local community. Let's consider two scenarios: a racist community, and a comfortable middle-class neighbourhood. A racist community may transmit values that offend other individuals who live in their society. This would be contrary to the aims and objectives of the National Curriculum and contrary to the aims necessary for a pluralist society. It would be a mistake for schools to imbue the values of the racist community in the spirit of reflecting the local ethos.

Let's now consider a cosy middle-class neighbourhood where the values are such that they wish to live in a gated community or relatively homogeneous suburb, have taxes benefit their local community and separate themselves from other poverty-stricken or racially mixed neighbourhoods. They live content within the confines of their local community, not bothering other socio-economic groups, but not assisting either. It may be arguable that schools may not want to reflect the narrow ethos of this community, but to expose children to broader issues such as diversity and social justice that are not promoted by that community.

While the intent of this statement appears to advocate that schools work in conjunction with the community respecting and reflecting the values of the community, the lack of clarity has potentially detrimental results. Without certain normative principles to help clarify and discern what particular forms of community we wish to promote, such statements can either be harmful or, at best, rhetorical.

The aims and objectives of the National Curriculum do little to help us conceptualize community. Instead, they provide general principles that are considered to be relevant and important to implement in schools. While the aims set a general tone, they do not offer much guidance or substantive clarity to the notion of community.

Schools and communities

Another key target area for community development is forging links between schools and their local community. Recent policy initiatives encourage community groups, businesses and members of the general public, to support schools. Some have become manifest in partnerships, and others through government directives (DfES 2003a). Similarly, schools are involved with collaborative projects in attempts to connect the local school to that of the external community as one of the objectives stated in the citizenship curriculum at Key Stage 4 (DfES 2003b). I address these various ways in which school–community linkages have been developed.

A recent directive linking community and business involvement in England to schools is that of the Education Action Zones (EAZs). In 1998, the Department for Employment and Education created 25 Education Action Zones. The impetus for this programme was to 'unite business, schools, local education authorities and parents to modernise education in areas of social deprivation' (DfEE 1997). Through involvement and financial commitment from community and voluntary sectors, the government EAZs' aim is to reduce the social and educational disadvantages found in lower socio-economic schools. Some of the strategies within the EAZs are to 'attract and retain teachers through incentives, smaller classes, and increased community participation' (Power and Whitty 1999: 543). The emphasis in this school/community link is not so much for students to feel committed to the community, but for the community to feel committed to schools.

EAZs are comprised of members from the local education authority (LEA), parents, members of the local community, voluntary organizations, businesses, other organizations (such as the Health Authority) and representatives from the schools themselves. The task is to raise educational standards of each participating school. EAZs are given more legislative flexibility to allow them to suggest innovative ideas that foster higher educational standards. To help this process, the DfES provides up to £750,000 funding each year with the expectation that £250,000 funding each year will be raised from the private sector (DfES 2002).

EAZs appear to have two focal points: 1. to raise the educational standards of the participating schools, and 2. to raise funding for the participating school. While each of the purposes stated here may be important and appropriate, the stated objective does not necessarily attempt to create a stronger communal relationship between schools and the community: it is rather a side effect at best. EAZs are thus a governmental initiative that attempts to bring the external community closer to the participating schools for the specific purposes of assisting in the raising of educational standards, and by raising funds.

Another government programme initiated in England is the Connexions partnership, which provides assistance to teenagers aged 13 to 19 to make a smooth transition from student to work life (DfES 2003a). It brings together various local agencies to provide guidance and support to students in relating to career, personal development and lifestyle. Personal advisors are located in schools, colleges and the community to connect with the teenagers. The hope is that the Connexions programme will support young people who have fallen through the cracks in the traditional educational system. The emphasis in this partnership is primarily to target disaffected youth, who may not have a smooth transition between school and work. The 'community' in this case is the working community.

Finally, one component identified in the skills and learning objectives in the Citizenship Curriculum at Key Stage 4 is that students will plan a community event (DfES 2003b). Three objectives are targeted as follows: 1. What skills do we need for effective teamwork? 2. Who are the key partners in the community? How can we develop effective partnerships? 3. How can we improve performance through critical analysis and evaluation? I will highlight the first two objectives.

The first objective requires that students should learn how to plan a project or event within their local community. This process requires that the student will learn how to participate as a member of a group, and it also requires some thought to an event that is relevant to the school and the local community. The examples that they cite include having a sports day, creating a multicultural festival within their community or hosting a Special Olympics day with students from a special needs school. They then suggest activities that will assist them in choosing an appropriate event, such as surveying the community for local agencies or conducting interviews with local residents. Finally, organizing the event considers the internal tasks that are to be undertaken in order for the event to be successful.

The second objective identifies a number of other skills that students are to acquire. The first suggests the skills necessary to work collaboratively to create a community event. The next identifies key partners in the local community who may be willing to cooperate and assist in their project. Finally, the third assesses how their project contributes to greater social change and enhancement for the school and the community. The key element in both objectives is that of participation and responsible action. Students must demonstrate that they have engaged with the local community. Schools are to comply with the objectives, and are evaluated by the degree to which they meet these standards (Ofsted 2002b).

These are but a few of the partnership initiatives that are currently in place in England. These examples illustrate the diversity and, perhaps, disjointed community directives that attempt to develop stronger links to schools and communities. Education Action Zones focus on economic partnerships from external sources; Connexions provide support to teenagers from local agencies; one component of the citizenship curriculum requires that students engage in the local community.

It is difficult to evaluate the effectiveness of each of these school and community partnerships, partly because they address different concerns, and partly because we do not know which features of community are important to foster. It may be the case that all of these partnerships serve an important purpose. We may, however, feel less comfortable if these community directives have unintended effects. We may, for instance, be concerned that Education Action Zones provide an unbalanced partnership with businesses and community members providing economic funds to impoverished schools, which have little choice but to join. Further, we may feel that, while the rationale for the programme is based on creating links between the community and the school, there seems to be little that makes this a community. Without any guiding principles to consider what we find valuable in communities, it is difficult to assess whether these various school and community partnerships are helpful or effective.

Community schools

Community schools have a prominent history in England. Prior to the formation of comprehensive state schools, many children were taught in numerous private settings, such as in the case of dame, ragged, charity, industrial or gaffer schools to name but a few. Lessons were taught often in houses of private individuals or local buildings, providing some level of instruction among the daily chores of the day. A mutual agreement would be worked out between parents and the teacher, offering flexibility to both the parents and the teacher in terms of when the children could arrive and depart.

Similarly, teaching methods and curriculum reflected local needs and circumstances. Because of the lack of resources in the school pedagogical needs had to be met within the community. Children were sometimes taken out of the schools and into the local community to study the natural world. In effect, the local community became their textbook (Gardner 1984, Higginson 1974, Stewart 1972). Despite the formation of monitorial and state-aided schools, many working-class parents criticized the pretentiousness of these schools, preferring dame and other private school teachers whom they considered 'persons in their own station of life' (Tropp 1957).

Similarly, much of the utopian movements of the eighteenth and nineteenth centuries often used education to strengthen the bonds of the community. One such example is the Owenite movement seen in both Britain and the United States during the early 1800s. Education was part of a larger Communitarian agenda in which utopian notions were embraced. The pedagogic directive was to foster a caring and nurturing environment, and teachers were discouraged from using a disciplinarian approach to pedagogy. Robert Owen, founder of the Owenite movement, hoped that teachers would spark the interest in the child and demonstrate that it was in the child's self-interest to foster the educated and civilized mind. Lectures were given by Owen and subsequent leaders to adults to foster the ideals of education through the community (Harrison 1968). Dialogic relations and associations were encouraged within the communes, and education would help to strengthen this community. For Owen, 'community education was a means of breaking out of the vicious cycle of social and moral degeneration' (Siraj-Blatchford 1997: x). Owen refrained from extrinsic rewards and, conversely, the use of punishment, and instead nurtured children's development through fostering knowledge within a collective, cooperative environment. The success of Owen's school in New Lanark, England is noted in a report of the Leeds Poor Law Guardians of 1819 which states:

In the education of the children the thing that is most remarkable is the general spirit of kindness and affection which is shown towards them, and the entire absence of everything that is likely to give them bad habits, with the presence of whatever is calculated to inspire them with good ones; the consequence is, that they appear *like one well-regulated family, united together by the ties of the closest affection* (emphasis added). (Podmore 1923: 148)

Although these utopian movements never lasted a generation or more, they provided strong community schools to reflect the ideals within the local community (Armytage 1961).

The influence of Dewey is also notable given his tremendous influence not only in the United States, but internationally for his strong emphasis on community and democracy at the heart of his notion of schooling. His philosophy forged new ways of thinking about how to educate children at the beginning of the twentieth century, from more traditional pedagogic practices to those that would be relevant and meaningful for the child.[1] In *The School and Society*, a large emphasis was given to how schools should be 'a genuine form of community life' representative of the larger society (Dewey 1977: 14). Schools, he thought, should not be a detached institution, teaching abstract and distinct subjects, but rather should imbue the values of the family and the local community. In this way, community was integral to his notion of schools, providing the social medium of integrating the child from the local parameters of the family and local community to that of the larger civic public sphere.

To develop children to their full potential, Dewey believed that education should be a place where children would cultivate certain habits, providing them with the necessary skills in which to negotiate their world. Habits would be learnt through positive, meaningful experiences provided in the school. Such learning experiences would help develop children's capacities to take control over their environment, and learn how to utilize it for their maximum potential. In essence, children would learn how to maximize the faculties of the mind and body through the connections and associations that were made in exposure to various experiences (Dewey 1915: 52–69).

Dewey grappled with this concept of the interconnectedness between individuals, communities and democracy. 'Fraternity, liberty and equality isolated from communal life are hopeless abstractions ... Democracy must begin at home, and its home is the neighbourly community' (Dewey 1984: 329). Communities are instrumental for democracy. If communities allow for multiple and diverse interests, and if communities encourage movement within and between multiple communities, communities can strengthen and support a pluralist democracy (Dewey 1997: 105). Dewey saw the potential of community to be a social medium that provided necessary connections between individuals and society. We cannot think of individuals as isolated from the world: such a perception does not acknowledge various interconnections, relationships and the general progress of growth. Every individual is part of a social medium and, as such, must have some reference to the values and meanings of the greater society. Communities are social mechanisms that strengthen the bonds between individuals needed to stabilize a democratic society.

While Dewey wanted to make significant connections to the greater community, he was also cautious of letting tradition and customs of the community simply govern the actions and mobility of individuals (Dewey 1915: 296). Blind adherence to custom does not encourage development, but rather stifles growth. Dewey wanted to ensure freedom for each individual. By freedom, he wanted to ensure a freedom of mental attitude and mobility to explore, experiment and to enlarge their understanding of themselves and the world around them (ibid.: 305). Dewey was committed to this ideal and promoted it both in his philosophical lectures and in his public life.

Dewey's emphasis on community values stems partly from his opposition to the impersonal, isolated transmission of knowledge to students. Dewey despised pedagogical practices that focused on individualistic methods devoid of social interaction and any motivation for learning. Having students sit in desks facing the front of a classroom during subject periods with no social interaction, and disciplined into passive forms of learning, was antithetical to the social aspect that would help to develop children's dispositions and mental capacities. Social interaction was a necessary condition for the growth and development of children.

Pronounced emphatically in his work, *Democracy and Education*, Dewey saw the importance for teaching the child how to be socially connected to others in the world. To begin, Dewey rightly notes that the terms *society* and *community* are ambiguous terms:

They have both a eulogistic or normative sense, and a descriptive sense; a meaning *de jure* and a meaning *de facto*. In social philosophy, the former connotation is almost always uppermost. Society is conceived as one by its very nature. The qualities which accompany this unity, praiseworthy, community of purpose and welfare, loyalty to public ends, mutuality of sympathy, are emphasized. But when we look at the facts which the term *denotes* instead of confining our attention to its intrinsic *connotation*, we find not unity, but a plurality of societies, good and bad. (ibid.: 82)

Dewey recognized that schools were one of the primary sites for socializing children through its aims and habits within a social environment. He also recognized the difficulty of weeding out the undesirable traits of community that suppress and limit growth, as opposed to those that broaden and open people up to multiple connections and associations. The difference was to limit those groups that wish to pursue only one ideology to the exclusion and suppression of other groups. The destructive element of such negative groups was that their survival and protection required the elimination and exclusion of other social relationships (ibid.: 85–6). To distinguish between negative and positive forms of community, Dewey used two forms of criteria:

How numerous and varied are the interests which are consciously shared?
How full and free is the interplay with other forms of association? (Dewey 1976: 105)

Vibrant communities are thus those groups that encourage both internal and external relations among its members. And while there may be a common aim of a particular community, divergent views and opinions by members are not only allowed, but encouraged to foster continual growth.

Despite the cautionary and worrisome aspects of negative communities, Dewey still had much faith in the promotion of community in schools. Schools, de facto, were but a microcosm of a larger community. Schools imbue community life in the social relationships among their staff, parents and students. In addition, the aims and objectives of a school create a certain community culture. What is it that we wish students to learn? What are the values that we wish to foster? What customs and habits are evident in the school life? Dewey pondered these types of questions in his quest for developing an educational theory that would guide us in establishing schools that would be to the benefit of children. Community, then, has a vital element in Dewey's vision of the educational system, and sought to capitalize on it for its potential for individual growth and understanding about oneself and others. He further saw the reciprocal nature of individual and community.

Schools, thus, are natural sites for developing the community spirit in children. We develop children's interests and perceptions through the common experiences found in the daily routines of school life. The school must further extend the conjoint experiences within the school walls to those outside of the school. The school becomes an extension to the broader community bringing the experiences of the outer world to that of the child. The child thus makes an easier transition from the close familial lifestyle to that of the school, and from the school to that of greater community: in doing so, the child learns to make continual readjustments and connections to society.

While Dewey's message created much discussion in American education (not to mention his influence in other countries such as China, Japan, Turkey, Russia and Western Europe[2]), critics pointed to the inefficient and unsustainable educational programme that he put forth. A large faction described Dewey's educational vision as particularly narrow, focusing primarily on the practical vocational element for a future workforce. Some saw Dewey's educational programme as economically unfeasible and highly inefficient. Others did not approve of the progressive educational element in terms of teaching to the interests and development of the child: rather, they simply wanted to hand down knowledge through the classics in return to 'back to the basics'. Finally, some could not see how Dewey could provide a balance between the liberal ideals of developing the child and the communitarian ideals of promoting the common good. Such lack of clarity exposed Dewey to much criticism for the ambitious, yet seemingly rhetorical and polemic nature of his work (see, for instance, Peters 1977). The ideals are grand and inspiring, but when asked for philosophical clarity or a 'template' for how these schools could achieve the social cohesion between the local and larger civic society, both appear to fall far short of their intended goals.

Despite this vagueness, Dewey warrants much merit for what one may consider his radical visions as to how we should approach education. He made us consider not only the relationship between the teacher and child, but also schools' roles in developing a democratic society. He challenged the traditional pedagogic approaches to considering how best we might foster the growth and development of the individual child to that of an active (and, I would add, autonomous) citizen in society.[3] Finally, he wanted to balance not only the autonomous interests of the child, but also saw the need to develop children's understanding of their communal dependencies and obligations that are part of a person's condition of living in a society. These ideals are both ambitious and commendable, especially given the time in which he lived, and the structure and aims of schooling common at that time. These basic principles have inspired educators to strive toward these broad normative principles and, as a result, still hold much resonance for educators today.

Another prominent figure to develop the notion of community schools was Henry Morris in his vision and establishment of the integrated-campus village and community colleges in Cambridgeshire and Leicestershire. Morris's vision sought an education that went beyond the confines of the classroom and the school (Rée 1985). For Morris, education had been an insular institution, remaining cut off from many valuable aspects of life and the community. His vision sought to conceptualize education 'so that it will be co-terminous with life'. In one of the writings that outlined the basis of his argument for the village school, he writes:

> We must so organise the educational building of the towns and countryside that the schools of the young are either organically related to, or form part of, the institutions in which the ultimate goals of education are realised. We must associate with education all those activities which go to make a full life – art, literature, music, festivals, local government, politics. This is as important for the teaching of the young, as it is for the teachers themselves. (Morris 1926 as cited in Rée 1985: 20)

Morris sought to remove the distinct barriers between schools and the community: the task was not only to teach the children, but also to provide an array of activities for the community that would enrich society as a whole. Morris's vision would provide much of the basis for contemporary community education, and continues to play a part in the English education system.

Rt Hon David Blunkett's speech entitled 'Raising aspirations in the 21st century (DfEE 2000a), identified four main factors for increasing community activities in schools:

- links with the community help schools in raising students' motivation, expectations and achievement. This leads to higher standards and improved behaviour. Support from parents and local community organisations can be a crucial factor in improving students' attainment and combating social exclusion;
- in many locations, the school is the main, or even only, place that can provide the local community with sports and other facilities. Using the local school as a centre for adult learning, childcare facilities and for meetings helps regenerate and strengthen communities. Schools can also support community learning and improving health;
- increased use of school premises can lead to improved security for the school site and reductions in vandalism and graffiti in the surrounding area;
- links with the community reinforce the fact that all education relates to the wider community and the world of work and professional practice. (DfEE 2000b: 1)

'Raising standards: opening doors', Report (2000b), based on the Blunkett speech, goes on to cite a number of successful community schools in Britain that have been recognized by Ofsted. It mentions Henbury Community Centre located in Bristol that has financial links with Hewlett Packard, British Telecom, Bristol City Council and the Single Regeneration Budget to provide up-to-date computer technology for students during school hours and for community members during the evenings and weekends (ibid.: 2). Cottenham Village College is a 'fully integrated community college offering full time education to 900 secondary aged students and community and leisure facilities to a population of around 10,000' (ibid.: 4). In both of these cases, substantial financial support is offered by businesses to support community initiatives.

Community schools hope to provide schooling to students and also to provide services to its local community members outside school hours. The school becomes a major site for community activity. The school is not segregated from the life of the community, but rather becomes integrated through extended community activities. In effect, the lines between schooling and education become blurred through the multiple and diverse activities that these schools offer during and after school hours.

Communities of interest

Unlike community schools whose purpose is to blur the lines between the school and community through shared use of facilities, educational programmes that have an expressed shared purpose or aim may consider themselves to be fostering community at the school level. Specialist schools, faith schools and 'choice' programmes all exhibit common features in that they have an expressed shared purpose that may enhance school community. Schools are formed around communities of interest: in other words, schools hope to attract like-minded students, parents and teachers who are committed to their educational mandate.

Specialist schools are schools that form a distinctive identity around a particular curricular area. The idea is that the expressed focus in a particular endeavour will lead to increased achievement success and an accelerated learning environment in that subject area. Each specialist school is linked to a private agency, and has connections to other partner schools. The schools are to share good practice and pedagogy in their identified area with non-specialist schools and in the broader community. Specialist schools are formed around the shared and expressed identified subject area. Students and teachers have shared interests and talents in the designated area in specialist schools. Currently, London has set a target of 290 specialist schools to be created by 2008.

Faith schools have a shared and expressed religious faith. The Church of England schools serve the Christian community. In a recent report chaired by Lord Dearing, Church schools are to promote and extend the Christian faith to families, and extend it beyond to others who share a common belief in God (Church Schools Review Group 2001). Although there is diversity among Church schools, the core values inherent in all are the 'gospel values in loving God and one's neighbour, as well as the practical outworking of these values in how students are taught to conduct themselves and relate to one another and to God's world' (ibid.: 19). Church schools are to: engage in meaningful acts of worship daily; have staff that are committed to the teaching of the Christian faith; reflect Christian faith; mark and celebrate Christian festivals; and maintain strong ties to the parish community. As the Archbishop of York notes:

The school is called to reflect these qualities: a fellowship and a community which gives individuals scope to be themselves, yet participating equally in the common life. Furthermore, to stress that the school is a community of persons (reflecting the Trinitarian life) is to emphasize relationships; the personal is thus prior to the institutional; the institutional does not exist for its own sake but solely for the purpose of nurturing and sustaining the relations of the persons who comprise any particular community or organization. (ibid.: 15)

The expressed purpose of faith schools is to bring students together in a Christian community.

Finally, 'choice' schools[4] offer an alternative educational programme that cannot be found within state schooling. Community members (often consisting of parents, community members and business people) may govern the boards of schools. Control of the school is given over to the school board members in terms of finance, management and daily practice. In return, schools are financially and educationally accountable: they must uphold the educational mandate (and often demonstrate increased educational student achievement) and be financially viable. Schools are often given three- to five-year contracts in which to meet the requirements.

Supporters of these educational choice movements believe that such schools provide students with an educational alternative that was not previously there. This extends beyond traditional neighbourhood boundaries in attempts to attract desirable students beyond the local geographical confines. The hope is to bring community members into the involvement of the local school through its governing structures. Schools hope to attract expertise from local businesses, and also to have a representative sampling of parents and local community members. In this way, schools aim to be more reflective and responsive to the needs and desires of their communities. Schools that have an expressed shared purpose often suggest a strong school community. Staff, students and parents share the values of the school. It is conceivable that these schools, in fact, do exhibit a strong sense of community.

However, other challenges may arise when we consider promoting schools around communities of interest. The first concern is the potential for exclusive forms of communities to increase. Schools may become increasingly selective with students who fit the criteria of the school, or may select students who are more desirable to teach. The second concern is whether having a particular shared aim in one school will encourage diversity between different communities who share a different belief. If one of the stated aims of the National Curriculum is to foster respect and diversity in the larger society, then the relative homogeneity of students in the school may not reflect this aim.

Although schools that have a specific shared purpose may effectively create a strong community in one sense, they may be detrimental to other communities that we find similarly valuable. Again, without an evaluative mechanism to distinguish how to mitigate competing values, it is difficult to distinguish which communities we should promote from those that we should not.

Community in the curriculum

Attempts to promote community are heavily cited in the Citizenship Curriculum in the National Curriculum of England, particularly at Key Stage 3. The general objective statement of the Citizenship Curriculum states:

> During Key Stage 3, students study, reflect upon and discuss significant aspects of some topical political, social and moral issues, problems and events. They learn to identify and distinguish the role of the legal, political, social and economic institutions and systems which influence their lives and communities. They learn about and continue to be actively involved in the life of their school, neighbourhood and wider communities and to be effective in public life. They develop skills, knowledge and understanding in these areas through, for example, learning about the key concepts, values or dispositions of fairness, social justice, respect for democracy and diversity; through study which covers issues at a range of levels, for example, school, local, national, global; and through learning in the community. (DfEE 1999: 1)

The objective statement for the Citizenship Curriculum has similar, recurring difficulties to that of the aims and objectives of the National Curriculum. For example, we can interpret the following statement in many ways, 'They learn to identify and distinguish the role of the legal, political, social and economic institutions and systems which influence their lives and communities' (ibid.: 1). We may consider the various social, political and economic institutions as particular forms of community, depending on one's definition of what encompasses community. We may further consider that 'community' in this sentence refers to a location: such institutions may influence our lives and the places in which we live. The other way in which to interpret it is that of community as a relationship: such institutions may influence our lives and the communities of which we are a part.

The second reference to 'community' is clearer: 'They learn about and continue to be actively involved in the life of their school, neighbourhood and wider communities and to be effective in public life' (ibid.: 1). Here, community is considered as a location, if one reads the statement that school, neighbourhood and wider community are all locations. However, what 'the wider community' entails is uncertain. It is probably assumed that a student's participation in the wider community at minimum means participation within the localities of which they are a part. However, participation in the wider community may be analogous to society. It is possible to conceive that 'the wider community' has undertones of civic responsibility.

The final mention of community suggests that students will learn certain dispositions in their interaction 'through learning in the community'. It assumes that the students' exposure to community is that of a healthy environment which will assist in the promotion of 'dispositions of fairness, social justice, respect for democracy and diversity'. Putting an emphasis on 'learning through the community' further assumes that students have experiences in communities that reflect positive dispositions.

The Citizenship Curriculum specifically addresses community in one of the units. 'Communities and Identities' is defined into three sections: local community, national identities and global citizenship. Each section provides key questions on which the section is to focus. They are as follows:

Me and my local community
- What are my identities?
- What groups/communities do I belong to and how can I contribute to them?
- What do I think about my local community?
- What concerns my community and who influences it?
- What is the diversity and difference in my community and how is it celebrated?

National identities

- How can different communities learn from each other?
- How do I understand diversity and how is it represented locally, nationally and globally?
- How tolerant am I of diversity and difference?
- What are the legal and human rights and responsibilities that underpin society?
- What systems protect and enable our rights and responsibilities?

Global citizenship

- Is there a global community?
- What organisations have a global role, accountability and significance?
- How do voluntary groups contribute to local and global development and understanding?
- How can I investigate and influence global issues?
- What is my role in a sustainable global future? (QCA 2001: 25)

These key questions guide the discussion throughout the unit, and highlight aspects of community that should be emphasized. Local community topics surround one's identity, contribution and celebratory aspects of participation. After completion of the unit, students should be able to recognize the various communities of which they are a part. Similarly, they should see the various ways participation in communities affects their notion of identity. Only one question, 'What concerns my community and who influences it?' has the potential to look at the internal mechanisms of the community, linking the common aims and purposes, and the power dynamics that may be prevalent in a community. However, the emphasis still focuses on the concerns of the community, rather than the concerns that an individual might have in a community. As such, the focus of the 'local community' unit primarily addresses celebratory aspects of being part of a community.

The national identities category focuses on group diversity and difference, with some acknowledgement of toleration. Two themes emerge in this section: the first theme concerns itself with teaching students an acknowledgement and acceptance of multiple types of community within a pluralist society; the second theme teaches students certain just preconditions that allow for diversity and toleration. Both themes overlap in that a society may require certain agreed-upon rights and responsibilities that provide protections for multiple and diverging types of community in a pluralist society.

The global citizenship section is more openly defined, asking questions of whether global communities exist and, if so, what are our contributions to and influence on such global orders. The first question, whether global communities exist, appears to be a rhetorical question based on the follow-up questions. The following questions ask the types of groups that contribute to the development of a global community through its interest in global issues. The final question then brings the individual into the discussion by asking what role each student plays toward a 'sustainable global future'.

Personal, Social and Health Education (PSHE) puts greater emphasis on the skills needed to become active citizens and form healthy relationships (DfES 2003d). One key objective is that students should learn how to play a role as active citizens. The focus lies on developing skills to discuss with others, learn how to debate, recognize key choices, agree to and follow rules implicit in relationships, and that they belong to various groups and communities. Another main objective focuses on how our actions affect others, in a spirit of respecting others' differences. Specifically, it teaches students to recognize how their behaviour affects others, to listen to others, to respect differences of other people, and how to mitigate teasing and bullying. Key Stage 4 PSHE builds upon the above skills to include students' awareness of exploitative relationships, and issues of prejudice and discrimination.

Three reasons are often cited for Community Studies/Service (CSS) appearing in the PSHE curriculum. First, children who are perceived as academically struggling may be able to identify with the specific activities within the community objectives. Hopefully, the relevance and interest in these activities will motivate children to do well in other subject areas, and increase their sense of responsibility. Second, students may develop a greater sense of empathy and concern for those less fortunate than themselves. Third, teaching about community in schools will provide benefits for society (Pring 1984: 134–7).

It is apparent that the intended benefits of promoting community are vast. Yet, whether or not such aims can be fulfilled is not clear. Chapters 8 and 9 consider school and societal conditions that makes the promotion of community difficult.

Norms and practices in schools

Some educators contend that it is difficult, if not impossible, to implement prescriptive solutions for schools in fostering community (Merz and Furman 1997, Calderwood 2000). Merz and Furman (1997) note several pitfalls in trying to mandate and bureaucratize a notion of community that will be applicable for all school contexts. By attempting to implement and employ strategies for enhancing school communities, what we may in fact be doing is creating certain educational settings that are 'more bureaucratic and less personal environments' (p. viii). They are consciously aware that large systems can produce many unanticipated ripple effects, which lessen the flexibility for schools to develop their own school culture to fit in with their unique social circumstances. Rather, they suggest an easing up with regard to mandating prescribed notions of community and allowing a bit of 'ordered chaos' to reign (p. ix). This is not only healthy, they suggest, but is also more reflective of the greater community that contends with the complexities of human social relations on a larger scale.

This view resonates with the idea that schools need to create their own meanings:

> The temptation to inoculate schools with community, if only one could, is strong. Community, however, is a slippery state of social relations. It is not a commodity easily obtained. There is no storehouse stocking tempting varieties and flavors of ready-made community, nor is there a warehouse filled with the ingredients that, when properly arranged, transform into community. Community gets built only as communities practice, and successful construction of resilient community is not guaranteed, even among the most dedicated group. (Calderwood 2000: 2)

This perspective suggests that educators promote community by embracing the lived and real day-to-day experiences of being part of community in school, recognizing that community is both 'vulnerable' and 'fragile' (ibid.: 140). Community, therefore, cannot be compartmentalized and packaged into a theoretical framework: community emerges through its members' participation in celebration and adversity, in their ongoing tribulations of what it means to be part of a community and in their ongoing deliberations about making a community work.

Informal social relations are often a strong determinant in

developing a sense of community in a school. What is still left to question is how such social relations are built and sustained, what level of flexibility and negotiation is allowed in the formation of social relations and who creates and influences the types of social relations that are to be formed? While Calderwood (2000) believes that the stronger communities show four common characteristics – group identity, accounting for internal diversity, ways to learn how to become competent and celebrations (ibid.: 140) – little mention is made setting constraints on particular types of community that may not be beneficial in schools.

Further, others consider how students and teachers construct themselves within the physical and contextual informal spaces of the school (Gordon, Holland and Lahelma 2000). Community may be defined *within* formal instruction times between students and teachers. Communities may also be formed *between* formal instruction, when individuals meet in the corridors, cafeteria and schoolyard. While the focus on communities has traditionally been set through formalized instruction or stated objectives, it is interesting to note that community can be formed in the informal spaces during school time.

Informal norms and practices may provide more meaningful communities that are shaped and developed by the individuals who are committed to the shared aims and purposes. These communities do not arise through stated aims and objectives, nor are they handed down through bureaucratic edicts, but they emerge as needs and interests are formed. The contextual daily experiences of individuals lead them to form communities that are suited to their needs and interests.

The ideals of informal norms and practices as a way to develop communities heuristically fail, however, to distinguish between communities that may be beneficial, inefficient or harmful. The emphasis celebrates the organic, grassroots formation of communities and neglects the difference between better and worse forms of community that may emerge in this contextual experience.

Conclusion

The prominence of community directives cited in education documents is noticeable. Promoting community is sited at all levels of schooling, and for vastly different purposes and aims. Principles are of a general nature: either referring to (perceived) dispositions *of* community, or encouraging students to participate *in* the community. Further, there is a distinction between developing links between schools *and* community, and fostering community *in* schools. In all cases, communities are considered *prima facie* good for individuals and society.

This premise is one that I do not take for granted. While it may be the case that some communities may be beneficial for students and societies, others might be far less so. However, this is not articulated in documents and therefore does not offer any protective assurances to mitigate harmful communities. Without some theoretical basis to evaluate communities we are limited to a haphazard approach of implementing various community directives.

To highlight why a random approach may be detrimental to individuals and society, I examine three problematic aspects of community in the following chapter.

Notes

1. In no way is this statement intended to detract from nor deny Dewey's many influences that shaped much of his thinking, most notably: the progressive educators, Rousseau, Pestalozzi and Froebel; the philosopher Hegel; and the sociologist, G. M. Mead.

2. Dewey lectured in each of these countries throughout his career, creating much stir, excitement and controversy for the ideas that he put forth in these countries (Ryan 1995). His extensive travels and lecture series drew large audiences and made a large impact both at the time that they were presented and in subsequent years, regarding how education should be thought about and addressed.

3. It should be noted, however, that while Dewey believed in a progressive education system that emphasized the development of the child, he was not in favour of child-centred education (an education system that lets the child decide and control the types of activities that will be cultivated, depending on the child's interests, wants and desires). Dewey thought this was ludicrous and was opposed to such ideas. The development of the child must take into consideration the child, but the child itself should not be in sole control of the type of education it would receive. Rightly, Dewey pointed out that certain habits and interests must be cultivated in the child for proper development to occur. At times, teachers may have to provide motivation and discipline in order to cultivate

habits beneficial for the child. Thus to make education relevant for the child did not necessarily mean that the child had
fee rein.

4. 'Choice' schools are labelled in various ways. Most commonly, they are called charter schools in the United States and
Canada, self-managing schools in New Zealand or the former
grant-maintained schools in England.

CHAPTER 3

Tensions Inherent in Community

While community is generally thought of as a good, community may also have negative aspects. The common concern is that collective rights of a group will supersede those of the individual. Yet, critics suggest that ensuring collective interests, especially those of a cultural or religious nature, may warrant certain protections (Kymlicka 1989), or even exemption of certain individual rights (Margalit and Halbertal 1994). Individual members may value these communities as part of the life they wish to lead, and thus deserve certain protections, especially those communities that are in the minority. To place individual rights before collective interests could potentially jeopardize the survival of a community, and thus decrease an individual's capacity to lead the life that he or she chooses.

I consider this debate between individual and collective rights, and argue that communities cannot be exempt from considerations of justice. I address three main problems of communities: dominant discursive practices internal to the community; exclusive membership in a community that disadvantages nonmembers; and dominant discursive practices that exert pressure on individuals outside the community. I examine each issue accordingly, identifying the problematic nature of certain community practices and apply these issues to current dilemmas in schooling. I then pose the question of whether or not it is better to promote 'community'. I conclude that what is needed is an articulated conception of community that addresses these concerns, rather than a complete denunciation of community.

Internal norms and practices

One conflicting aim of community may be those group norms and practices that infringe on individual rights within a community. The debate between individual and group rights within a community is not new among theorists; however, this issue becomes more complex and problematic when addressing children and, more specifically, their status as dependent members of that community. Central to this concern is trying to balance the right of parents to raise their children in a particular tradition with that of the state interests to protect children within the boundaries of justice. A common way to mitigate the tensions between individual and group practices internal to a community is to suggest protections that allow individuals to enter and exit a community. Given the dependency of children, I suggest that this is insufficient to address internal dominant practices that may inhibit children's present and future life prospects. Let me outline the basic argument between the infringement of individual rights within a community, before considering the question of children. In doing so, I will briefly outline when (and if) the state is justified in intervening in parents' rights to raise their children in a particular way.

In a liberal democratic society, states generally do not interfere with parents who are raising children in a particular tradition and way of life.[1] People belong to various communities that provide a sense of belonging or, more substantially, a sense of identity. Parents may wish to pass down their religious, political or moral beliefs to their children, all of which seem reasonable and acceptable. The difficulty lies when communities may infringe on the life choices of some members. Women, for instance, have commonly been marginalized in various community practices both historically and contemporarily. How then do we distinguish between community practices that provide a certain quality of life and value to its members and those community practices that may infringe on basic individual rights? States that intervene in the private spheres of the community may be accused of imposing their values on communities that place greater priority on other values than individual rights: simply put, they may be regarded as being 'heavy handed', imposing 'Western ideals on others', or taking on Orwellian 'Big Brother' tendencies.

These accusations are ones that I do not share. While states should take great pains to respect and encourage multiple ways of living, allowing people to flourish in their respective communities, it also seems reasonable to contend that a threshold level be attained and guaranteed in order to protect those vulnerable members within a community. Nussbaum (2000) suggests that basic universal philosophical principles need to be guaranteed by all governments to ensure a basic minimum of 'what respect for human dignity requires' (p. 5). It is not enough to allow collective interests to override basic primary rights of individuals. Although it is one thing to be culturally sensitive to local practices, it is another to suggest 'general values, such as the dignity of the person, the integrity of the body, basic political rights and liberties, basic economic opportunities, and so forth, are not appropriate norms to be used' (ibid: 41). Allowing communities to instil practices that are physically and mentally detrimental to an individual, or states to exempt communities from the basic considerations of justice, are mistaken. Let me explain why neither scenario is appropriate.

One apparent reason is that the basic fundamental rights of an individual are necessary for a person's well-being. Without basic fundamental rights, individuals are constrained in their ability to lead the life of their choosing. If we are denied access to schooling, maltreated, oppressed or unable to voice our opinions and concerns, individuals have little hope of being able to change the circumstances of which they are a part. Their efforts are limited to attaining basic needs and, arguably, they lack the capabilities to change their circumstances effectively. Similarly, leaving it up to states to determine whether or not to interfere in community practices allows the potential for oppressive practices to continue should states not have an incentive or desire to interfere. For instance, states may not alleviate the problem if it is to their advantage to sustain oppressive practices or, simply, if the powers of authority are themselves corrupt (Nussbaum 2000: 41–70). Fundamental rights to individuals are non-negotiable and are essential to every person's life. Allowing communities to pursue oppressive practices in the name of collective interests, or states preferring not to interfere, are both unacceptable options.

Second, dominant practices of a community are often enforced on vulnerable members (Okin 1999). Let us consider an extreme example – that of female circumcision. Female circumcision is usually practised on adolescent girls. Adolescent girls are vulnerable in at least three ways: they are not adults and may be limited in their ability to consent or resist; their economic opportunities (that of entering marriage) may be bound together by the practice of female circumcision; and there may be extreme pressure from members of the community and family, for some of whom they may have great respect (Okin 1999). To suggest that these adolescent girls have the capacity to resist the internal practices of that community is unrealistic. It is difficult for vulnerable members to resist dominant practices and authority figures in the community. The oppressive practices create vulnerability and reduce the possibility for an individual to intervene, resist or change practices not of their choosing.

Third, where there are established norms in a community, those members who are subject to practices may lower their own expectations to that of the accepted practices. 'Unjust background conditions deform people's choices and even their wishes for their own lives' (Nussbaum 2000: 114). For instance, a girl who is not allowed to attend school may not even consider opportunities for employment. In these cases, members who are manipulated or oppressed may adapt their preferences to match the dominant norms of the group. The capability to pursue or revise the choices they wish to have in their life is reduced greatly if they recognize that they do not have the requisite skills or support from their community members to pursue their interests. Dominant repressive practices increase the likelihood of members having adaptive preferences.

For example, when a number of Hutterite members decided to leave their religious colony in Canada, they were not permitted to take any personal possessions or material wealth from the colony. Despite their challenge in court, the Court supported the collective rights of the community (*Hofer v. Hofer*, [1970] S.C.R. 958). They would have little to no financial independence, they may have few skills or capacities to leave a community upon which they are dependent and may have to overcome marital and communal obstacles. Individuals who are subordinated by the dominant practices of a community will take great risks to free themselves financially, mentally and physically. The greater the infringement of these rights, the more difficult it is for those members to exit a community.

When we consider internal collective ideals that conflict with individual protections for children, we add a considerable amount of complexity to the problem. Unlike adults, children do not have the same ability to enter and leave a community. Children are, for instance, bound by where their parents (or caregivers) choose to live. They are further often initiated into practices of a community to which their parents belong. Unlike adults, children may not have the developed capacities to understand, negotiate and act upon what is in their best interests as to participation in a community. They are dependent on their parents, guardians and other members within their community.

Finally, exempting collective interests from considerations of justice fails to protect members *within* that community. The ideal of protecting the practices that are perceived to be necessary for the survival of the community overshadows protections of actual members who are part of that community. Gutmann (2003) highlights a case whereby a Pueblo woman was denied residency rights, voting rights, rights of tribal membership to her children and other welfare rights as a result of her interracial marriage to a Navajo man. The woman was denied full membership rights within the Pueblo community – a community in which she had grown up and considered a cherished part of her identity. The woman challenged the community to retain full membership rights in the Pueblo community for herself and her children, and was heard before the United States Supreme Court. The Supreme Court ruled in favour of the Pueblo community, in not inter-fering with the self-government of the tribal community. 'To abrogate tribal decisions, particularly in the delicate area of membership, *for whatever "good" reasons*, is to destroy cultural identity under the guise of saving it' (*Martinez v. Weinberger*, 475 US 503 (1986) cited in Gutmann 2003: 46). The Supreme Court felt that they had to respect the collective interests of the com-munity, despite their uncomfortable stance regarding the Pueblo woman.

While the intention of the Supreme Court was to protect the community interests of the Pueblo community, Gutmann (2003) points out the irony that, in protecting the collective interests of the community, they actually failed to protect the interests of particular members within that community. The Pueblo woman felt attachment and loyalty to the community. She did not want to exit the community, but wanted to embrace the traditions and practices of the community. Her only challenge to the accepted norms of the community was that she married interracially. The result is that the Supreme Court supported the *established authorities* within the community, and did not protect the interests of all of its members within that community.

To mitigate the problem of dominant internal practices, liberals sometimes suggest guaranteeing entry and exit procedures for individuals. Kymlicka (1989) suggests that liberal states need to protect collective group rights because belonging to a cultural membership may be a primary precondition for an individual's sense of identity. For a state not to protect the interests of a group would greatly hinder and impinge on one's identity if that community were to dissipate. He thus advocates external community rights. However, Kymlicka acknowledges that individuals need protections that allow them entry and exit procedures within a community. Should individuals wish to leave a particular community, they have the ability and right to do so. Community rights cannot impose internal restrictions on individualism and, in this way, attempt to reconcile internal collective values with individual protections, by ensuring entry and exit procedures.

The difficulty with this position is that it assumes that all individuals can actually leave the community should they so choose. However, this may be an overly optimistic position. The more basic rights that a community infringes upon some of the members, the more difficult it is for vulnerable members to exit a community (Gutmann 2003: 61). Consider that dominant members of a community may restrict schooling to some or all of its children, may restrict women's economic opportunities or may create other major obstacles that inhibit their exit.

These concerns are of particular concern for the state, and thus for schools. What role should schools play in respecting tolerance and diversity of various cultural communities to that of protecting the interests of a child? Should schools place certain constraints and limitations on the internal practices of a community that limit a child's present and future opportunities?

A frequently cited case that elicits this complexity is that of the Old Order Amish community in the United States. The 1972 *Wisconsin v. Yoder* case (406 US 205) considers whether compulsory school attendance infringes on the religious freedom of parents to raise their children in the Amish way of life. The Amish faith seeks to return to a simpler life, de-emphasizing material success, renouncing competitiveness and insulating them from the outside modern world. They argue that the Amish children's integration with other children in the modern world, and learning the curriculum that emphasizes science and technology would seriously threaten their continued and accepted way of existence. For them, survival of the Amish way of life warrants limiting their children's attendance in public education. Parents therefore want the ability to remove their children from schooling following the eighth grade. The Supreme Court of the United States agreed, and exempted Amish children from compulsory attendance laws after completion of the eighth grade.

Two legal questions are generally used to assist in these rulings: the threshold question and the balance question. The threshold question considers whether the contested practice constitutes a substantial burden on the free exercise of religion. The balancing question considers, assuming a burden exists, whether state interference should outweigh the burden of free exercise (Reich 2002b). The Supreme Court decided that the Amish children who attended state schooling would substantially compromise the cultural integrity of that faith community. They further thought that it did not warrant state interference to force Amish children to go to state schooling. It should be noted that the verdict might have been considerably different if the Amish families challenged that their children not attend *any* state schools. The Amish provided a compelling case that the children would attend primary education until the eighth grade. Further, they guaranteed that the children would still receive education within the Amish community, reflecting the skills and training needed for their agricultural way of life. Finally, those skills developed in the Amish community could be transferable to skills outside of the Amish community and, in this way, should the teenagers wish to leave the Amish, they could find suitable alternative forms of work within the modern world (*Wisconsin v. Yoder*, 406 US 205).

However, in another educational court case, a similar challenge made by a Christian fundamentalist group did not attain a similar favourable ruling. Bob and Alice Mozert were members of a Christian fundamentalist group in Tennessee. They challenged the Hawkins County Board of Education claiming that the Holt reading series, a required reading series text for children, was offensive to their religious beliefs, and asked that their children should not have to read from the reading series. The Holt reading series is a series of texts used by children from grades one to eight. The readings are integrated into various courses throughout the day, and are used not only to improve literacy competency, but also to develop critical reading skills. The material that the Mozert family found offensive included aspects of evolution and 'secular humanism', and less familiar themes of 'futuristic supernaturalism', pacifism, magic and false views of death (*Mozert v. Board of Education*, 827 F.2d 1058). If their children continued to be exposed to the reading series, the Mozert family sincerely believed that they would damn their children to eternal hell, and their parents for allowing their children to read the series (Reich 2002b).

In this instance, it would seem that the request by the family was less severe than the *Yoder* case in that they did not want their children exempt from compulsory schooling, but simply to refrain from reading the text series and they requested alternative readings. However, the District Court of Appeals did not award the *Mozert* family an exemption from the required reading series. The Appeals Court felt that the burden on the free exercise of religion would not unduly threaten the survival of the religious community. The basal reading series did not propagate a particular view, and instead only exposed children to various viewpoints. The court believed that this exposure was not a significant burden that would interfere with the parents' freedom to practise their religion. The threshold question did not hold. As a result, the Appeals Court did not address the balance question, as it was dismissed on the first point.

These examples make explicit the tension that schools face in trying to balance respecting community ideals to that of protecting the autonomous interests of the child. In modern pluralist society, we assume that schools will foster respect and diversity in schools. We also want schools to protect the interests of each and every child, and to cultivate certain skills and dispositions to be fully functioning members of society. Without normative principles to assist us in these difficult circumstances, it is near impossible to suggest how one might resolve these dilemmas.

Principles of justice are an appropriate regulatory device for curtailing certain community practices that may infringe on a child's present and future life prospects. Guaranteeing that the basic rights of children are not infringed upon is not a moral ceiling, but a necessary assurance for their future life prospects. While the principles do not provide a particular conception of community to offer for schooling, they do provide a way in which to justify when certain internal community practices may be detrimental to a child. In so doing, multiple types of communities may still be fostered in schools (and between schools and their communities) within these parameters.

Exclusivity and community

Individuals belong to voluntary communities in that they can enter a community where there is mutual identification and shared commitments. Exclusive membership of a particular community ensures that its members not only share similar common aims, but also have the ability to fulfil their aims with like-minded individuals. Survival of a community may require that its members espouse common ideals, and that these are of a selective nature in which to achieve its ends. Under freedom of association, liberal societies allow communities to be exclusive and selective in respecting diversity and toleration. This is the general position taken by liberal states to protect communities in their rights to freedom of association and freedom of expression.

We can think of numerous scenarious where exclusive membership in a community might be reasonable and acceptable Various religious doctrines have varying degrees of exclusivity. Some religions such as Orthodox Judaism require that membership can only be achieved by being born into the faith by parents who are Jewish. It is not possible to convert into this particular faith. Fraternities and sororities among American college campuses are other exclusive private communities that select potential undergraduate students who will match the ideals of their members and their mission statement. Similarly, unions and guilds are selective in that the community is defined by its common aims within their profession. To have members outside this practice may alter the aims and objectives of such communities.

However, if some individuals wish to join a community, but are denied access due to discrimination, they are denied their freedom of association. Communities that deny access to particular individuals due to prejudice – against their gender, race, ethnicity or sexual orientation – may disadvantage those individuals and deny them opportunities to belong to a community and the benefits that community may accrue to its members. For example, many business lodges historically denied women access in their clubs. Business associations may provide individuals with considerable networking connections and the potential to create business deals during the club activities. The denial of admittance of women into those business associations would mean that women would lose out on the opportunities and benefits of being part of that association. The dilemma addresses two competing values: the freedom to form an exclusive group and the freedom not to be excluded from a group based on discrimination (Gutmann 2003: 88).

Various exclusive communities are also found in educational practices, varying in degree in the selection criteria of its membership. Elite schools that enrol only those students who excel in academic work, sports and performing arts may have very exclusive admittance policies. Admittance criteria may be based on the student's demonstration of a particular talent that is considered to be at an exceptionally high level for a particular age group. These elite schools may target and obtain students who show remarkable present talent and future potential in a particular skill.

Other schools may wish to create a particular community ethos by having a set mission statement to which students and parents must abide. In order for a student to gain admittance to a particular school programme, the student and parent must agree to the school mandate. The hope is that schools will find students who match their community's ethos, and select students based on their suitability to the schools, common aims and objectives.

Similarly, single-faith schools often set criteria for student enrolment into their schools. Faith schools are often set up in three ways. Some schools may set policies only to accept children who come from families who are active members of their faith. Other faith schools may have a policy to have preferential enrolment for students who are active members of their faith, before allowing access of other families who may not share the same faith, but who may choose the school for other reasons. Finally, some faith schools may have an open enrolment policy that allows all students, regardless of their faith, to be admitted to their school. The enrolment policy of various faith schools shows the varying degrees of selection that are considered and used.

The controversy of allowing selective practices of membership into a particular school community raises a particular dilemma of whether selective communities create certain positional advantages for some students to the disadvantage of other students. Various school choice reforms may fall under this category, setting up various school mandates to create a particular 'school community' (especially those that are unregulated and market driven). If an important educational aim is to provide both equitable conditions and opportunities for children in order that they have an equitable footing in later life, then selective school communities may conflict with educational equality.

In some cases it may be acceptable to have selective community membership within a particular school. For instance, we might see little difficulty with a school for the deaf that has special resources allocated to their specific needs. Such a school would provide the necessary support needed for those children to maximize their full potential and, further, would not be to the disadvantage of other children. Deaf children may require more resources and special instruction in order to have an equal footing with other able children in later life. It is thus reasonable to argue that the special attention and resources given to deaf children would not necessarily disadvantage other children, but would provide them with more equitable opportunities to lead a good life comparable to that of other children.

By increasingly allowing schools to have more power to choose their student membership, one potential outcome is that students who are more difficult to teach and who may thus require more funding to meet their needs may be excluded from particular schools (Gewirtz 2002). Under a veil of developing a strong school community ethos, exclusionary practices can emerge through student admittance polices.

How can we distinguish between schools that require a selective student membership in order to fulfil their particular mandate, and those schools that may wish to develop a strong community by limiting the types of students who can enrol in their school? In both circumstances, schools contend that they require a selective student population that will allow them to fulfil the common aims and objectives set by the school. Is it sufficient to accept that so long as school communities maximize the full potential of students enrolled they are justified in selecting students for enrolment? Must the role of the state, including public education institutions, be to consider what the repercussions of exclusive school communities might have on other students who are excluded? A tension therefore exists between providing a strong community ethos in schools through the process of selective student membership and ensuring that all students have a fair opportunity to receive quality education that will provide students with an equitable footing in later life.

Dominant community practices toward non-members

The final tension arising in the promotion of community is how to balance dominant community practices that may infringe on the rights of individuals who are not part of that community. This tension centres on the issue of whether it is acceptable in certain circumstances to allow group rights to take precedence over individual rights. Are there circumstances where dominant community ideals may warrant the infringement of individual rights of those who do not share those ideals?

In extreme cases, it is easier to resolve this position where community rights infringe on non-members under the considerations of justice. For instance, it is unacceptable for a white supremacist group such as the Ku Klux Klan to put undue pressure on visible minorities by intimidating them or causing them physical harm. This is a relatively straightforward dilemma of protecting individuals from oppressive community practices. Other examples may prove more difficult to resolve when limiting certain individual rights may protect minority groups.

Kymlicka (1989) argues that individuals have a primary right for individuals to have access to cultural membership. He states '(1) that cultural membership has a more important status in liberal thought than is explicitly recognized – that is, that the individuals who are an unquestionable part of the liberal moral ontology are viewed as individual members of a particular cultural community, for whom cultural membership is an important good; and (2) that members of minority cultural communities may face particular kinds of disadvantages with respect to the good of cultural membership, disadvantages whose rectification requires and justifies the provision of minority rights' (ibid.: 162). To ensure this, Kymlicka suggests that external protections for cultural communities are acceptable in order that they can be sustained and fostered within the larger plural society. While this may place certain constraints and limitations on other individuals to ensure these group rights, Kymlicka believes that cultural membership is an important good, and should be protected by the state.

Such external protective measures do exist in some places. Quebec, Canada, is one such example that protects the French culture and language under provincial laws. Surrounded by a dominant Anglophone culture from the surrounding provinces of Canada and the United States, numerous policies have been employed to ensure that the French language and culture are not assimilated by the surrounding dominant English culture. Bill 101 requires all commercial signs to be written in French. Store owners whether they are French or non-French must abide by this law. Similarly, families who emigrate to Quebec are required to send their children to Francophone schools. They do not have the option of sending their children to an English-speaking school. The rationale for such laws is that, because English is such a dominant culture surrounding Quebec, it is necessary and acceptable for the state to put certain constraints on non-French-speaking individuals in order to protect the survival of the French community in Quebec.

Is constraining certain individual rights reasonable in order to protect group interests in an educational context? Is it acceptable to require all children to learn French even if they are not of French origin? Recognizing that in Canada French and English are the two official languages, one might argue that this Quebec law is unacceptable in forcing immigrant parents to send their children to French schools. Conversely, we might state that the survival of the culture depends upon new immigrants accepting and embracing the French way of life. It might therefore be a reasonable condition to require immigrants to foster the French way of life, including sending their children to French-speaking schools.

In the example whereby parents in Quebec are compelled to send their children to French-speaking schools, we see that the French culture is given more weight and protection than the individual wishes of parents who might choose to send their child to a school other than French. In this case, the debate centres on whether the protection of the cultural community warrants the restriction of individual rights. This raises a thorny dilemma of whether in certain circumstances group rights take precedence over individual needs and wants. In examining the balance between protecting dominant community ideals and that of protecting individual student concerns, we may need to consider the burden that it places on the individual and whether it is a minor burden as compared to something much more serious.

Most people recognize that dominant practices that infringe on the rights of other non-members in society are unacceptable. Protecting minority cultures through collective rights that affect non-members, however, is a more difficult issue to resolve. Deciding the criteria for what collective rights are to be protected, who should be protected and to what extent they should be protected, is difficult to assess. Further, this needs to be balanced with the effect that this has on individuals who are not part of those communities.

Should we dismiss the notion of 'community'?

Some suggest that 'community' conceals and represses discourses of power (Rose 1999). In an age of third-way politics, Rose (1999) speculates that community may be yet another power structure through a form of governance. In the last decade, both the Clinton, Bush and Blair administrations have tried to use 'community' to create supposedly neutral spaces to govern under the label of community. This is seen in the growing proliferation of community organization schemes and outreach projects. According to Rose, community has the potential to be the 'constitutions of new forms of authority', and the 'instrumentalization of new forces in the government of conduct' (ibid: 189). Community has become the new valorized form of authority that can lay claim on concepts such as the 'black community' or the 'local community' (ibid.: 189). While community is often seen to promote commonality, emotional support and solidarity, there is the potential to ignore and suppress aspects of community that produce effects of assimilation and normalization. What is required is to consider community from a larger discourse that addresses 'moral regulation, emotional management, and political practices that normalize forms of participation and specify particular relations among people' (Fendler 2001: 2). The problematic aspects of community may warrant a hesitant approach to promoting community in schools.

At the other end of the philosophical spectrum are libertarians who find themselves oddly in agreement with postmodernists in their suspicions of community (although posed differently). Libertarians are also wary of community in its restriction of freedoms that communities may and do place on the individual. Community can place considerable pressure on individuals to conform to practices and beliefs held by the collective status quo. A libertarian perspective puts utmost priority on the liberty of the individual. This manifests itself in two ways: liberty is a central value to be protected by governments, and liberty is a primary right of individuals. The main purpose of the state is to ensure that individuals are not forced to do anything not of their choosing unless the constraints placed on individuals by the state specifically protect the liberties of other individuals. State involvement should be limited to only protecting negative rights: the protection of individuals from external obstacles or interference (Nozick 1977). In this theory, community could be at odds with libertarian aims. Community places particular burdens on individuals' freedoms, especially if individuals are asked to follow and conform to certain practices and beliefs.

Equally worrisome for libertarians is the way in which individuals are expected to pursue some common good *for* the community as if community takes on a life of its own (Jasay 1995). Appeals to promote some collective good without explicitly stating its particular benefits to its members within the community are troubling. It is not surprising then that libertarians do not attribute high value to community, and would prefer to see curtailment of its promotion in education and in society

Both views are partly correct in so far as their critiques expose the dangers of promoting community. Community can infringe on certain rights of individuals. Further, community can take on anthropomorphic tendencies whereby the communal life is valued above and beyond the individual (Dworkin 1989: 492). It is not assumed, therefore, that community is beneficial for individuals, and may warrant more healthy scepticism before promoting it in schools.

Can a normative theory mitigate tensions found in promoting community?

In this chapter, I have examined three tensions that arise between community and individual rights. The first tension addresses internal community practices that infringe on the rights of its members. The second considers the tension arising when community practices exclude individuals from entering voluntary associations due to discrimination. The third examines dominant community ideals and practices that infringe on freedoms of non-members. Finally, I pose whether it may be better to dismiss the notion of 'community' due to its problematic aspects.

Each concern has relevance for schooling. Internal community practices that limit a child's present and future opportunities conflict with liberal educational aims of fostering autonomous individuals in state schools. Exclusive school communities may provide distinct advantages to some students but, in so doing, may disadvantage those who are not selected to be part of those communities. Finally, dominant community practices that infringe on non-members raise questions about the balance of protecting collective rights against the burdens that those traditions may place on children. Left undefined and unaddressed, these tensions may give schools problems in finding a solution. Policy statements and curricular objectives place strong emphasis on promoting community values in schools. Yet little attention is given to resolve the tensions in community when they may conflict with competing values.

In articulating these concerns, one solution might be not to promote community in schools. This tendency to disregard community, however, is unwarranted. Rather than a complete denunciation of community, what is called for is a more careful philosophical conception of community that is mindful of these concerns.

Before I articulate a philosophical conception of community, I will first outline some reasons to support why community may be valuable for individuals and society. I now turn to reasons that support a notion of 'community'.

Notes

1. One may be sceptical about the accuracy of this statement. Some may believe that the state has tremendous influence over individuals and their communities. However, to acknowledge that this may not be such an innocent generalization, let me make two brief claims. One might believe that I am referring to countries such as the United States or the United Kingdom: let me be clear that the non-ideal realities of both countries may be far from the ideals of a liberal democratic society. Second, I will refer to Rawls' ideal vision of a well-ordered society, whereby the basic structure of society – that of political, economic and social institutions – are governed by a theory of justice. In turn, the principles of liberty and equality guarantee varying conceptions of the good within people's private spheres. This will be developed more thoroughly in Chapter 5.

CHAPTER 4

Valuing Community

Why is it that people have such strong attachments to the notion of community? Rarely, do people come out and say that they do not believe in the notion of community. However, what do people mean when they say that they value community? Do we all mean the same thing when we talk about community? What are the similarities, and where do we diverge?

Different weight and value is given in our conceptions of community. In its most basic form, community is simply a domain of human communicative interactions with others: our relations with friends, neighbours and fellow workers create networks and linkages. At the other end of the spectrum, community is an inescapable, constitutive part of one's identity. Finally, community promotes a shared sense of belonging or a common ethos through individuals' commitments and attachments to a group. All three conceptions overlap, but their different emphases lead us in potentially radically different directions in our reasons for promoting community.

I highlight these three perspectives and consider their relevance for promoting community. In the first case I suggest that, while interacting with others is part of the human condition, it is a weak conception of community, which does not require any deliberate action to develop. The second case, that of a constitutive community, while potentially valuable for individuals, is one that I will not endorse due to the inability of persons to revise or reject their attachments to a constitutive community. Instead, I endorse a conception of community that is based around individuals' sense of shared belonging and identity, which allows individuals to develop and exercise their judgement in belonging to or refraining from community. This conception of community allows for flexibility in individuals' formation of communities, in their ability to participate in both thick and thin communities, and in their ability to pursue and revise their participation in communities throughout the course of their life.

Following this discussion, the second part of this chapter cites common reasons for promoting community based on individuals' sense of identity and belonging, and the concomitant benefits it may have both for individuals and for society.

Communities are domains of communicative interaction

Humans are communicative beings. Humans do not live in isolation: they are dependent upon others from the moment they are born into the world. Children develop and learn from the environment of others. Individuals live together and increase their social connections with others through their participation in various relationships. This basic human function of interacting with others forms the basis of community.

This is not a new or surprising notion. Aristotle's starting point is that humans are political animals. Humans, unlike any other life form, have the ability of speech and reason (*Pol.* I.2 1253a7–18).[1] As such, humans' ability to communicate their feelings, what they believe to be just and unjust, good and evil, etc., makes them different from other species. Humans are in contact and already connected to others around them. 'To not have such contact or reason would make us savage and uncivilised. Luckily, man [*sic*] is naturally inclined to participate in the affairs of reason. To communicate with others and act in ways toward their betterment is not only a natural tendency, but is virtuous' (*Pol.* I.2 1253a29).

The basic function of interacting involves an aspect of sharing in the experience of others, 'We know about one another, enter into each other's concerns, rejoice at others' happiness and grieve at their pain' (Miller 1998: 229). Our conceptions of our selves are bound up in our interactions with others and, in this way, individuals are an integrated part of a larger community.

This basic conception of community focuses on the natural tendency of humans to interact with others. It does not require deliberate action, but is an integral part of being human. It is, however, a thin conception of community, emphasizing human interaction, rather than on any 'thicker' shared aims.

Communities are constitutive of the self

At the opposite end of the spectrum is the belief that communities are constitutive of the self. This position suggests that, when individuals are born, they are born into a particular culture, experience and language: all of which encompass a tradition. Individuals are not able to choose the type of culture or tradition to which they wish to belong. Communities already form our identity, without our conscious or informed consent – it is already present and a part of us.

MacIntyre contends that the self is attached to others, inextricably, not of our choosing. Our relations with our parents, our siblings, cousins, neighbours and communities are not something from which we can detach ourselves but constitute who we are as persons (1981: 32). We identify with communities, and our community identifies us. This interwoven relationship with others partially or wholly defines us, and the reciprocal responsibilities and duties that come with these social practices.

Similarly, Taylor (1985) believes that it is impossible to understand the self as separate from one's interpretations: selves are partly constituted by an interpretation, and only progress towards wider interpretations (or understanding) starting from that position. The self is able to interpret and broaden one's understanding, but it is partly already constituted by a certain interpretation. The self begins as a social self-interpreting being. We shape our understandings, but the understanding has partly shaped the self (Taylor 1985: 27). Further, in order to shape and expand our understandings, we must have a language in which to express such thoughts: a language that is already formulated by certain beliefs and foundational structures. These foundational structures are not of a singular nature that can be determined by one person, but they are inter-subjective, meaning that they are based on a social and practical reality (ibid.: 37). The self is therefore rooted in social practice and cannot be separated from it.

Bell (1993) develops the notion that the socially embedded self is vital to one's identity: to attempt to escape or detach oneself from one's constitutive community would damage the person. Defining how we are part of a constitutive community comes from the basic question of how we define ourselves or, simply put, 'Who are you?' (Bell 1993: 103). Many people will define themselves based on place, race or ethnicity, or a combination of all three. These form the bases that become the foundations of our fundamental identity as a person. According to Bell, to attempt to disown or disavow a part of our constitutive identity would cause tremendous psychological damage to the self, being devoid of 'meaningful possibilities' (ibid.: 100). Bell identifies this state as 'damaged human personhood', which can put people into acute disorientation (ibid.: 101). For instance, the way in which we are brought up in a community accords such weight to our identity that to break away completely would cause tremendous emotional distress. People who disavow their constitutive community, in effect, disavow a part of themselves. According to him, it is both unrealistic and damaging to have such a highly individualistic notion of the self; rather, we need to embrace an embedded self which provides moral grounding upon which to give us guidance and moral foundation in our life (ibid.: 184).

For many people, identity is not shaped by a notion of a separate and detached self − it is shaped by language culture and social practices − a person's identity is formed by living in their communities. To what degree identity is shaped by community, and to what degree there is flexibility and malleability in terms of individuals' abilities to make decisions about their life (that is contrary or resistant to the community practice to which they were inducted) is a matter of debate. At one extreme, Bell contends that to disavow one's constitutive community would be detrimental to one's well-being. Taylor, however, suggests that, although we have a starting position as socially interpreting selves, we can make decisions that will influence and shape our identities throughout our lives.

It is not problematic that individuals find value in constitutive communities. The problematic aspect in this conception is that proponents of constitutive communities assume that individuals cannot revise or pursue alternative ways of living apart from the community into which they are born. In order to secure children's abilities to make informed judgements and choices about how they wish to lead their life, both in the present and in the future, the constitutive community cannot be endorsed, especially in the strong position of Bell. We can still allow individuals to belong to communities that are valuable to them. Fostering a community that does not permit individuals to exit their constitutive community neglects the problematic aspects of community that I raise in Chapter 3.

Communities promote belonging and attachment

A common reason for valuing community is that it fosters a greater sense of belonging and commitment among its members. Communities may provide a sense of belonging for individuals without any necessary accomplishment or achievement (Margalit and Raz 1990), communities may benefit members who share and develop similar interests in a supportive environment (Gutmann 2003), and communities may provide validation and worth to individuals who know that others share similar values (Kymlicka, 1989).

The first argument outlines the positive benefits that people may derive when they have a sense of belonging to a community without having to prove themselves. This form of community may be described as being an ascriptive community (Gutmann 2003). People are identified *by* their community through an identifiable trait or characteristic – be it skin colour, ethnicity, race, gender and the like – among its members. This is different from people who have a conscious mutual identification of a shared aim. For example, cultural membership of a community may not require an individual to excel in a particular endeavour or be successful. Margalit and Raz (1990) make this point when they state, 'To be a *good* Irishman, it is true, is an achievement. But to be an Irishman is not' (emphasis added, pp. 446–7). Membership of this type is determined by who that person is, not by what that person does. For many, having an 'unearned' entry into a particular community is a valuable aspect of their lives (Gutmann 2003: 42). Having a sense of belonging through cultural membership may provide security and safety whereas many other communities may have specific criteria for acceptance into their group.

The second argument addresses the positive effects that people derive when they voluntarily choose to be part of communities that share common values. Mutual identification by its members is a key element in associative communities (Gutmann 2003). We identify with people who share a common interest or aim, and identify with other people who feel a reciprocal commitment and attachment. Communities help people to have a sense of belonging with like-minded individuals who want to pursue common goals and aims. It is both reasonable and important to consider promoting community for the purposes of developing people's interests and values. Communities therefore serve the interests of their members by providing a supportive environment that allows for individual flourishing.

Supportive communities can also be mutually reinforcing environments, fostering individuals' sense of self-respect and worth. Self-respect is important because it provides meaningfulness to an individual's course of action and life activities. Communities may help to orient people's sense of self, and provide direction and meaning to their life choices and plans (Gutmann 2003: 42). For instance, the early struggles of the civil rights movement in the United States were often started by the resistance against certain practices by one or a few individuals. However, as it gained in strength and through community, there was a reassuring and validating aspect that others were of the same view, and that they could come to together in solidarity.

This form of validation in community is often associated with providing a voice to individuals who share common values. A strategic and empowering aspect can occur when individuals come together in community through the increased influence and power in the collective strength of belonging to a community to raise a particular issue. Feminists, minority groups and deliberative democracy advocates may feel that their voices can be better heard if they form a larger collective to raise issues within the public sphere. A collective community can often raise the profile of a particular issue due to the sheer number of people committed to the project, compared to an individual who tries to forward her view and finds her voice difficult to be heard (metaphorically speaking) against other dominant discourses in society (Phillips 1995, Young 2000, Gutmann 2003: 8–12). Communities can be an effective means for change.

Communities can thus provide a sense of belonging and self-worth in many respects. In the first case, it is important to acknowledge that people find value in belonging to a community, through some form of recognition by other members of that community. Voluntary forms of association provide the second major way in which people are attached to others. Finally, communities that come together for a specific cause, such as the civil rights and feminist movements, provide validation to people's thoughts and ambitions by reinforcing their views through solidarity.

Individuals make choices about what practices they choose to become involved with that are valuable in their lives (Kymlicka 1995: 83). Communities may facilitate this process. Religious communities may give shape to a person's sense of identity – they may come to appreciate and believe the accepted traditions and social practices inherent in the community. Particular communities, those of ethnicity, race and religion – are very strong conceptions of community that may be influential in a person's life. Many people will affirm and accept the society and culture of which they are a part, having an intimate attachment to it. These strong conceptions of community contribute to many people's sense of identity. People thus value their participation in many communities because they provide 'an anchor for self-identification and the safety of effortless secure belonging' (Margalit and Raz 1990: 448).

An important aspect for many people's lives is that they can identify with their communities. Ensuring that people can identify and create a sense of identity through the communities ensures a freedom of choice and a freedom of expression for individuals. Protecting individuals' abilities to pursue the types of communities that will facilitate their identity is an appropriate guarantee in a liberal state. Individuals should be able to participate in a community, especially those that provide them with a sense of identity, without fear of discrimination or punishment.

The key characteristic is an individual's sense of belonging and commitment to others who share common aims and interests. It is the *ethos* that people find valuable in belonging to a community that is pivotal.

Purported benefits of belonging to a community
Given that individuals find meaningfulness in their participation in communities, other benefits are often ascribed to individuals' participation in community. I consider some common reasons cited for promoting community and corresponding perceived benefits.

Dispositions of care and reciprocity
Communities may develop dispositions of care and reciprocity. While care and reciprocity can conceivably be learnt outside of community in daily interactions with other people, communities may be effective social mediums that provide conditions to develop enduring relationships. Aristotle (1953, 1962) suggests that individuals partake in relationships that will be of some benefit. We enjoy the company of others, and we enjoy the compassion and love from someone not only so that a person feels love, but also to reciprocate it. These activities are an active realization of pursuing the good life. Our moral obligations and

responsibilities to those for whom we have a particular affiliation and affection may bring out an ethic of care and concern for others more than in less communal relationships.

The ways in which we develop an ethic of care is realized in several different ways (Noddings 1984). We may care for someone out of responsibility or obligation. Our attention towards an elderly person who requires assistance is one form of care. We may care for someone who has regard or inclination for someone or something. A person may care about a relative who holds some special significance for that person. And, finally, care may have some charged feeling or concern for the welfare and protection, or maintenance for someone or something. Individuals may care about the environment or about the protection of civil liberties. All of these aspects of care can arise out of daily informal inter-actions with others; however, sustaining long-term relationships that are common in communities may be conducive for solidi-fying and reinforcing feelings of care and concern for others. Kerr (1996) writes:

> Social spaces, civic spaces, a safe, shared place to play with life as one actually experiences it; a place where others recognize, acknowledge, respect one's experiences – the self requires these and is constituted in them. One finds one's self, then, not by retreating to the solitude of ponds, mountains, gardens, or deserts. Those may be places to go to clear one's head, but they cannot provide the wellsprings of the soul. (Kerr 1996: 47)

For Kerr, nurture is developed in the communal spaces in public life. Our care for others is in the embodiment of our communal surroundings: in our friends and family, neighbours and com-munities. And sharing implies the most basic form of trust: it involves elements of vulnerability in opening up to other, and having a reciprocal element of care between two people (ibid.: 48). These forms of intimate, caring communities, however, must be tempered with democratic principles between autonomous selves built on respect, trust and self-respect (ibid.: 53–5).

Similar to the notion of care, communities may instil the virtues that withstand the test of time. Virtues are not a whim of the self, but lie at the core of a good society. Such virtues are the pre-requisites of a good person, and the prerequisite for a good society, and thus guide us in our practices and our relationships to others (MacIntyre 1981: 200–1). We learn such virtues through social practices embedded in community life. These practices help to form a narrative of which we become a part, changing and evolving, yet embodying the past (ibid.: 181). We do not learn about developing positive virtues in an abstract manner: living in community teaches individuals about care, courage, justice and honesty. Individuals are inducted into the traditions of a community, and through the learning of accepted social practices.

Tam (1998) argues that common values cross cultural differences and moral traditions. Tam identifies four values, those of love, wisdom, justice and fulfilment, which underpin all communities and provide the foundation of 'deeply valued human experience' (p. 14). Although Tam recognizes that these may not be the only values that are held commonly among cultures, they are at least the pivotal values of which individuals must assume responsibility and duty to uphold and protect. To deny or detach oneself from these values would cause tremendous conflict and hostility among various individuals and groups. It must therefore be a priority and obligation to ensure that such values are protected and upheld. For Tam, communities are the appropriate place in which to nurture and foster these values.

Putnam (2000) argues that there is a strong correlation between individuals who are active in community life and those who tend to display more altruistic acts of kindness and reciprocity. For example, he states that community members are often more willing to help out in informal situations such as assisting in the aftermath of a natural disaster or simply by watching a neighbour's house (ibid.: 120).[2] Reconnecting to community, in as far as it is vibrant and inclusive, has the potential to build strong dispositions of care, trust and reciprocity among its citizenry.

So community is a social medium through which individuals are able to learn positive dispositions about care and welfare for others, and reciprocity. We do selfless acts because we know and have come to have a special obligation and concern for another person. These relationships help to solidify these dispositions within the close social network, which can then transcend and transform into greater general acts of kindness in the broader public sphere.

Communities that develop dispositions of care and reciprocity are of value to the members of that group. They provide internal goods to its members. However, communities that foster care and reciprocity may also have benefits for non-members and the larger society, depending on the community's purpose. For instance, a community whose purpose is to support a charity will provide goods to non-members within that society.

It is important to note that not all communities develop dispositions of care and reciprocity. Chapter 3 makes clear that many communities may not promote care or reciprocity, but, for instance, narrowness and insularity. In considering the promotion of community for schooling, it would be necessary to distinguish those communities that foster care and reciprocity from those that do not. This will be developed further in Part II, assessing which communities may better provide dispositions of care and reciprocity, and constraining those that do not.

Communities are instrumental for a just society

A long-standing philosophical argument has been to show that the stability of society depends on an active and strong communal presence among its citizens. Aristotle notes that it is not enough to live in close proximity to be a community. Living together merely to protect against certain injustices does not make community. Nor does living together for the mere sake of creating necessary transactions make community. 'The state is an association intended to enable its members, in their households and the kinships, to live *well*, its purpose is a perfect and self-sufficient life' (*Pol.* III.9 1280b33–35). We form relations with others because we choose and want to live together and associate with others. This in turns helps us live well.

To ensure a just society, it is argued that citizens must share the responsibilities of ruling or being ruled. Such a constitution will promote the virtue of men [*sic*] in order that they neither rise above other people, or that such positions are not determined only by luck or natural ability: such shared reciprocal responsibility reduces the possibility of tyranny and the potential for an unjust state that privileges certain people over others (*Pol.* IV.11 1295a25–33; *NE* V 1129a21–b6). Ideally, citizens will form, contribute and benefit from political community in their commitment to create a just society (Curren 2001: 135). For Aristotle, community is part of the larger political community. We form certain associations to pursue common aims and goals: for Aristotle, this is the pursuit of the good life. We further form communities for mutual benefit such as pleasure, protection and transactions. In forming such relationships, Aristotle's ideal is that communities provide a sense of justice together with friendly feeling (*NE* VIII 1159b25–1160a9).

The claim that communities provide a social good for society places certain obligations and duties on individuals in contributing to society. Taylor (1985) resists individualist theories that fail to take into account the potential for collective forms of association. He contends that the atomistic quest for one's personal conception of the good life fails to account for larger collective issues, specifically those collective issues that do not directly nor necessarily affect one's personal goals. What a primacy of rights fails to take into account is individuals' belonging and obligation to a society (Taylor 1985: 188). To sustain a society requires more than just a protection of personal rights: it requires a reciprocal duty to adhere to certain authorities, established through our consent, for our collective advantage. Primacy of rights, or atomism to which Taylor refers, requires the self to be self-sufficient and independent of a polis. This is both untenable and unrealistic as we are inextricably social animals tied to others. This will not help us determine what goods we should further in society as a collective body (Taylor 1995a: 186). Taylor suggests that we enjoy security from a variety of public services such as a police force, fire department and national defence – all of which require some level of social responsibility by their citizens (ibid.: 190).

The foundation of a just society requires communicative associated living, and communities may be instrumental in bringing individuals together. However, this claim relies on the assumption that communities will bring people together and work collectively toward common aims of society. This may be true. However, it does not acknowledge power differentials in communities and between communities. It further requires people not only coming together in their own community, but also working with individuals outside their community. The claim that communities are instrumental in providing an active citizenry and a just society are contingent upon these conditions that I have noted.

Communities develop greater trust and social capital in societies

Some correlate individuals' participation in communities with greater trust and social capital in society. This claim contains four aspects: shared norms and cohesiveness of a community builds trust among individuals; individuals, who have ongoing relationships in communities, have greater social capital than those who have fewer connections to others; individuals who have greater social capital will engage in more civic activities than people who have less social capital; societies benefit from greater levels of trust and social capital in society. I will consider each of these claims in turn.

The first part of this claim is that communities develop greater levels of trust. The correlation is that individuals who interact with others repeatedly over time have a greater stake in developing relationships built on honesty, trust and reliability (Fukuyama 1999, Bowles and Gintis 2002). Our common norms can be formed based on 'thick' shared understandings, such as a belief in God, but they can also be formed on weaker conceptions, such as one's professional relationships and behaviours to fellow workers (Fukuyama 1995: 26). Further, it is to the benefit of members to know others' characteristics, behaviours and habits if they are likely to share future endeavours with them (Bowles and Gintis 2002: 424). High-trust societies, in turn, help to secure healthy economic environments in certain ways. Organizations built around high levels of trust do not have to implement so many bureaucratic rules, safeguards and procedures: accepted norms of practice and behaviour regulate the workplace (Fukuyama 1995: 26). Communities often have implicit norms, by which to enforce certain practices, either through peer pressure or mutual monitoring. Communities enforce a strong form of reciprocity in this sense (Bowles and Gintis 2002: 425). Further, societies that have high levels of trust and social networks will better adopt new practices that suit changing needs and circumstances (ibid.: 30). In sum, communities may 'more effectively foster and utilise the incentives that people have traditionally deployed to regulate their common activity: trust, solidarity, reciprocity, reputation, personal pride, respect, vengeance, and retribution, among others' (ibid.: 424).

The second part of the claim is that individuals who participate in communities have greater levels of social capital than those who do not belong to communities. Social capital varies in degree according to one's involvement in communities. At the first level, individuals who participate in a community, usually within their own culture or religion, may have a support network within that community. Not every membership in community will necessarily create social capital; rather the practices in the community must be based on cooperation, mutual commitments, reciprocity and the like (Fukuyama 1999: 2). A Jewish or Mormon community may exhibit strong levels of social capital, providing strong bonds between members of that community, and help in each other's prosperity.

The next level of social capital consists of individuals who not only belong to one community, but also are involved in multiple and wider communities. This increases that individual's social capital in developing further networks and relations beyond their local community, and may broaden the individual's experiences and insights. In this way, participating in multiple communities assists in developing ongoing relations and interactions with other people from diverse backgrounds. Moving beyond the internal cohesiveness of a community to building more connections to others outside of the community strengthens the social fabric of society (ibid.: 8). Having moral obligations that extend beyond the local confines of a community to multiple groups increases the social stability of society.

The third claim follows from parts one and two. Individuals who participate in communities are more likely to become involved in other public matters. This is an empirical claim arguing that there is a correlation between one's community involvement and responsible civic activism. Putnam suggests that individuals who belong to organizations, especially to religious organizations, are more likely to be philanthropic. He argues, '87 per cent of members of secular organisations and 76 per cent of members of religious organisations made some charitable con-tribution, as compared with only 37 per cent of non-members' (ibid.: 120). Individuals belonging to religious organizations give a larger percentage of their annual household income than those from secular organizations. He then goes on to show that com-munity members are twice as likely to donate blood compared to those who are not active in the community (ibid.: 120). Putnam acknowledges that these are indicators of social patterns of society, and do not necessarily prove his claim; at best they may indicate trends in social patterns of people's behaviours and levels of par-ticipation, while recognizing other reasons for people's level of participation in public matters.[3]

Putnam believes that it is an empirical matter that those who are more connected increase the 'channels through which we recruit one another for good deeds, and social networks foster norms of reciprocity that encourage attention to others' welfare' (ibid.: 117). It is a virtuous cycle. To make this point, Putnam suggests, we need simply to look at the parent who becomes involved in the Scouts due to the child's interest in the organization. That parent may be asked to help out at a local charity event, and at that charity event another person asks if that parent could help out with another community event. The parent, in effect, becomes known for their participation and willingness to become involved, and thus becomes part of an intertwining web of social activities. 'Volunteering fosters more volunteering, in both formal and informal settings' (ibid.: 121).[4]

The claim that communities foster greater trust and social capital is correct under specific conditions. Communities may play an instrumental role in encouraging individuals to become active in collective issues. Communities, however, can be a liability for a society if the community practices create a gulf between members of a community and those on the outside. Increased social cohesion of a society may increase if individuals belong to several communities, considering multiple interests and forming multiple and overlapping relationships. Strong bonds within a closed community, that disadvantages others, are not a basis for wider social capital (Fukuyama 1999).

The need for communities

Community is valuable for several reasons. The reasons range from aspects of belonging and attachment, to forming one's identity. Similarly, community is often considered as a social good, developing dispositions of care, reciprocity and trust – all of which may have potential positive implications for individuals and society.

Combining the concerns of community noted in Chapter 3 with positive reasons for its promotion, we can now move on to develop a philosophical conception of community within the considerations of justice. In Part II, I develop normative principles that both assist in evaluating communities, and are valuable for individuals and societies.

Notes

1. 'References to Aristotle's work refer, in accordance with scholarly norms, to the book, chapter, page, column, and line numbers of Immanuel Bekker's 1831 edition of the Greek text of the extant works. Hence, (i)Pol. IV.15 1299b24–25 refers to (i) Politics, book four, chapter fifteen, page 1299, column B, twenty-four through twenty-five.' (Curren 2000: xiv).
2. See Kaniasty, K. and Norris, F. (1995) 'In search of altruistic community: patterns of social support mobilization following

hurricane Hugo', *American Journal of Community Psychology*, 23, 447–77.

3. For example, Putnam does note other patterns of individual participation in the public sphere that do not necessarily originate from community alone. Persons with children, high levels of income, level of education and employment, size of the community, are all predictors of the level of individual participation in public affairs (p. 119).

4. Evidence cited for this claim can be read in Wilson and Musick (1997, 1999), and Wilson and Janoski (1995).

PART II

Developing a Liberal Conception of Community

CHAPTER 5

A Liberal Conception of Community

Having considered the potential negative effects of community in Chapter 3 and the purported benefits of community in Chapter 4, I now wish to develop a normative argument for promoting a liberal conception of community. This chapter will show how Rawls' liberal theory fosters certain communal dispositions necessary for social justice, and ensures protections of various communities under this political structure. After I have developed the philosophical principles upon which to evaluate permissible communities in a plural society, the subsequent chapter will show how these principles can then be applied to educational contexts.

Community and liberal theory functions at two different and distinct levels within Rawls' liberal theory: the first level addresses the macro structure of the overarching political organizational structure known as the basic structure of society; the second level considers the myriad communities that are nested within this political structure. Rawls defines this as 'a union among social unions' (Rawls 1985: 241). The basic structure of society is the primary subject of justice for Rawls and, through its instantiation of the principles of justice, it realizes a distinctive vision of community. But within this overarching structure, many less inclusive communities exist – neighbourhood associations, churches, schools, community groups, religious sects, etc. – whose formative influence on citizens' lives may or may not be in keeping with the principles that characterize the inclusive societal community.

As such, the first half of the chapter will consider the implicit aspects of a liberal community within the overarching basic structure. I begin by considering how the principles of liberty and equality provide an evaluative mechanism for considering communities that are to be constrained within liberal theory. I then consider the fair system of social cooperation and the notion of reciprocity, which is a necessary and assumed precondition of Rawls' two main principles.

The second half of the chapter is devoted to understanding the second layer of communities underneath the overall political structure. Specifically, I wish to examine Rawls' idea of the burdens of judgement and its corresponding ideal of toleration within the boundaries of reasonable pluralism. To address the dilemma of what constitutes 'reasonable pluralism', I will attempt to clarify various degrees to which communities may fall within reasonable pluralism. By making distinctions within Rawls' notion of reasonable pluralism, I develop a set of normative principles that discerns and promotes particular communities within a liberal society.

I have purposely chosen to draw on Rawls' political theory in order to develop a liberal conception of community. I suggest that principles of justice can be applied to develop normative principles that protect communities that are acceptable and desirable within the limits of reasonable pluralism. Basic rules of conduct protect reasonable communities in society through the ideal of toleration, and constrain others that go beyond what is permissible in a pluralist society. Basic principles of justice protect individuals within communities. While the principles I develop for community are Rawlsian in spirit, the conclusions extend beyond Rawls' central task of developing a distributive theory of justice.

Principles of liberty and equality

Rawls' liberal theory is based on the premise that 'justice is the first virtue of social institutions' (Rawls 1999: 3) His political theory, based on social justice, is the primary mechanism for ordering the public political culture. How we come to define and create acceptable rules and behaviours is developed through Rawls' theory of justice as fairness. Rawls' theory addresses two main principles of justice, that of the liberty principle and the principle of equality (to whom Rawls refers as the 'second principle'):

(a)   Each person has the same indefeasible claim to a fully adequate scheme of equal basic liberties, which scheme is compatible with the same scheme of liberties for all; and

(b)   Social and economic inequalities are to satisfy two conditions: first, they are to be attached to offices and positions open to all under conditions of fair equality of opportunity; and second, they are to be to the greatest benefit of the least-advantaged members of society (the difference principle). (Rawls 2001: 42–3)

The two principles guide us in setting basic rights and duties accountable to the basic structure of society – those of political, economic and social institutions – and, in turn, they provide appropriate principles based on the liberal ideal of free and equal persons. Basic liberties that are protected include 'the right to vote and to hold public office, freedom of speech and assembly; liberty of conscience and freedom of thought; freedom of the person; ... freedom from psychological oppression and physical assault and oppression; the right to hold personal property and freedom from arbitrary arrest and seizure as defined by the concept of the rule of law' (ibid.: 53). Liberty principles have lexical priority over principles of equality: simply, basic liberties are to be upheld over and above issues of equality when conflicts arise between the two principles.

The second principle contains two parts. The first part considers fair equality of opportunity, in that positions of office and power are accessible to all. The second part, referred to as the difference principle, states that social and economic inequalities can only be justified if they are to the greatest benefit of the least advantaged members of society. Fair equality of opportunity has lexical priority over the difference principle. The lexical priority is one that is debated among liberals, and one that I will not address here, other than to acknowledge that it is far from assumed or accepted.

Rawls advocates a political theory based on the central tenet of free and equal persons (Rawls 1993: 3–4). By limiting liberal theory to a political conception, Rawls wishes to avoid debating the merits and weaknesses of controversial religious, philosophical and moral doctrines, upon which it may be difficult for people to agree.[1] In an increasingly pluralist society, it is difficult to achieve consensus based on a comprehensive moral doctrine. He states, 'I should like to avoid, for example, claims to universal truth, or claims about the essential nature and identity of persons' (Rawls 1985: 223). The principles of liberty and equality provide the basis for Rawls' political theory.

This does not mean that other virtues or dispositions are not helpful in strengthening and improving a society; rather other virtues, while important, fall subordinate to principles of justice. Rawls states:

> As citizens we have reasons to impose the constraints specified by the political principles of justice on associations; while as members of associations we have reasons for limiting those constraints so that they leave room for a free and flourishing internal life appropriate to the association in question. (Rawls 2001: 165)

Rawls is sensitive to the fact that people may have different conceptions of the good life. An important value for people is to allow them to form, pursue and revise the way individuals choose to live their lives. Only when comprehensive doctrines infringe upon liberty and equality must they be constrained by justice. In this way, Rawls attempts to create a political theory based on reasonable pluralism.

Community, then, has a place in Rawls' political theory. So long as community adheres to the principles of justice, liberty and equality, community can have a valuable place in people's lives. Pursuing and revising one's conception of the good may involve belonging to, participating in, and identifying with aspects of community. Similarly, our devotions to and affections for other people and various communities is an important part of the human condition, and one that requires protection. These are valuable aspects in many people's lives, and one that Rawls acknowledges. Principles of justice ensure that people have this capability within the boundaries of reasonable pluralism. What is considered to be within the parameters of reasonable pluralism will be considered in the final section of this chapter.

In the next section, I will consider the preconditions upon which Rawls' political theory rests.

A fair system of social cooperation

Rawls's *a priori* assumption is that fundamental ideas are implicit in the public political culture of a democratic society. He suggests that the public political culture is one that is based on a 'fair system of cooperation over time from one generation to the next' (ibid.: 5). Simply, this means that individuals will be cooperating members of society as free and equal persons (Rawls 1993: 20). Secondly, principles of justice are ongoing and transmit values in society from one generation to the next. He acknowledges that this is an ideal position, but does so in order to remain focused on his central task of developing a political theory. It is the assumption of cooperating members of society that I wish to explore in greater detail, and which suggests an implicit notion of community in liberal theory.

The idea of social cooperation is a pivotal concept under-pinning Rawls' theory. The idea has three aspects:

(a)   Social cooperation is distinct from merely socially coordinated activity – for example, activity coordinated by orders issued by an absolute central authority. Rather, social cooperation is guided by publicly recognized rules and procedures, which those co-operating accept as appropriate to regulate their conduct.

(b)   The idea of cooperation includes the idea of fair terms of cooperation: these are terms each participant may reasonably accept, and sometimes should accept, pro-vided that everyone else likewise accepts them. Fair terms of cooperation specify an idea of reciprocity, or mutuality: all who do their part as the recognized rules require are to benefit as specified by a public and agreed-upon standard.

(c)   The idea of cooperation also includes the idea of each participant's rational advantage, or good. The idea of rational advantage specified what it is that those engaged in cooperation are seeking to advance from the standpoint of their own good. (ibid.: 6)

I argue that these three conditions of social cooperation are linked to the idea of community. Specifically, I argue that community is *instrumental* and *essential* to Rawls' ideal of social cooperation; and, if community is essential for social justice, then to a certain degree, it will be *constitutive*. Let me begin by expanding upon the instrumental and essential arguments in more detail, and then seek to show how community is implicit in the idea of social cooperation.

Firmly entrenched in this idea, is the requirement that persons must have at least a minimum level of social interaction with others. Rawls' liberal theory assumes that people will be rational and reasonable in coming together to determine a set of fair and just principles to regulate society. It requires individuals to acknowledge, consider and propose principles that will be acceptable to all.

The second aspect of Rawls' social cooperation addresses reciprocity and mutuality. The idea of reciprocity is that persons will be willing to accept certain principles that are agreed upon, even if they may not be to their personal advantage, so long as others do the same in order to maintain social justice in society. This differs from the notion of mutual advantage where individuals derive personal benefit from a particular situation. There appear to be at least two implicit components in the idea of reciprocity: one, is an inherent trust that others will comply with the principles; and two, that by complying with the principles even if they may not affect me personally or may even be to some disadvantage, is nonetheless beneficial for a just and stable society. Social cooperation in this instance has a collective purpose attached to it: I will agree and accept the principles knowing that it will be to the greater, public benefit of society, so long as others agree as well.

The last feature of Rawls' notion of social cooperation entails that it must be to each participant's rational advantage, or good (ibid.: 6). This is a protective assurance to ensure that participants are not constrained without their consent, nor are they being coerced into a practice they do not accept or are not comfortable with. Certain rules and procedures should not be to a person's detriment against their will, nor should it suppress certain individuals for the advantage of others.

Communities are instrumental to social cooperation

Community may be instrumental in creating conditions that are conducive for developing social cooperation. The first aspect of social cooperation requires that a) people come together, and b) that they cooperate under publicly recognized rules and procedures of conduct. This assumes that people are reasonable and rational and that they will interact with others in forming the guiding principles for rules of conduct in a society. People who have common aims or shared purposes may be more likely to come together and cooperate than those that do not. Communities can be instrumental in satisfying the basic criterion of the first point.

Similarly, implicit and explicit recognized rules of conduct are prevalent in communities. It seems reasonable to suggest that it is easier to learn how to cooperate and set out particular rules of conduct when one participates in a community, rather than if the person is detached or isolated from others. That, I suggest, can be learnt through their participation in community. This can be simply illustrated by observing an only child in a family who then must learn to cooperate in a larger social setting. The exposure to and participation in various communities helps to assist the child in learning how to cooperate and negotiate fair procedures that are acceptable in larger groups.

The second aspect in social cooperation is the notion of reciprocity. Communities often have strong elements of reciprocity: people come together for some shared purposes or beliefs, and often will do 'their part' as members because they believe that the collective interests may be of greater benefit, which in turn benefits the cooperating individuals. Considering the interests of others, and understanding the reciprocal benefit that communities may have for its members is often a strong indicator of stable communities. Again, communities may be instrumental in demonstrating the benefits of reciprocity.

The third aspect, that of rational advantage, actually does not support the idea that communities are instrumental, but provides a vital protective feature for individuals in communities. Communities that infringe on the rights of individuals – such as exploitation, intimidation or oppression – cannot be justified under the terms of social cooperation.

I have argued that in order for persons to learn how to be socially cooperative, community may be instrumental in learning such dispositions. Conversely we see liberal theory provides protective measures to mitigate adverse effects of communities that are not to individuals' rational advantage. Communities that exploit and infringe on the liberties of individuals can be constrained within a liberal conception of community.

Communities are essential to social cooperation

I now wish to argue that community may be essential to liberal theory. If the basic structure requires social cooperation as a precondition for a just society, I suggest that community is a necessary condition in which to foster social justice. This is a strong claim in that not only is community instrumental to social cooperation, but social cooperation can be achieved only through one's involvement in community.

The first aspect of social cooperation, as defined within Rawls' theory, involves publicly agreed-upon principles to help regulate accepted forms of conduct. Rawls explicitly states that social cooperation is not mere socially coordinated activity. This process of coming to agree upon such principles involves two aspects: first, the process entails people interacting with others to develop such principles; second, developing agreed-upon rules and procedures involves individuals interacting for a shared purpose, or a common aim. Social cooperation cannot be achieved through having the mere presence of people together, nor can it be achieved through issuing edicts from some higher authority.

The process of individuals coming together to pursue a shared purpose such as setting up rules and regulations by which to abide already entails being part of that community. The fair system of social cooperation as Rawls points out entails more than socially coordinated activity. It is a more onerous task, one that is conscious and deliberate, and may require ongoing relations and interactions. This, I suggest, is different from one's daily informal interactions with people. It involves a deliberate social cooperation as cooperating members of society. The process of people coming together for the expressed purpose and aim of creating publicly recognized rules and procedures already implies participating in a community. Further, once those rules and regulations are established, the community does not dissolve; rather, the accepted rules of conduct create part of a particular conception of community. Community becomes an essential aspect of social cooperation.

If community is a necessary condition of social justice, then in some limited capacity one could argue that community is *constitutive* of liberal theory. This is a precarious step to take, since Rawls explicitly argues against combining a notion of community with his political theory. He states his reluctance to consider community with his political theory at the beginning of *Justice as Fairness*:

> I believe that a democratic society is not and cannot be a community, where by a community I mean a body of persons united in affirming the same comprehensive, or partially comprehensive, doctrine. The fact of reasonable pluralism which characterizes a society with free institutions makes this impossible. This is the fact of profound and irreconcilable differences in citizens' reasonable comprehensive religious and philosophical conceptions of the world, and in their

views of the moral and aesthetic values to be sought in human life. (Rawls 2001: 3)

In reading this, one might assume that Rawls would have little to do with community, and would feel perhaps even hostile to my claim that liberals need to have a conception of community within their political theory. But let me explain. The point of contention, as stated by Rawls, is that he purposely does not want to promote a community that has a unified, or partially comprehensive doctrine. Yet, could we not think of Rawls' reasonable pluralism as a particular political community? Let me try to address these questions and hopefully, in so doing, suggest that community is constitutive of liberal theory.

The fear, for Rawls, is attempting to find a political doctrine that will be acceptable to varying religious, philosophical and moral doctrines and thus by all citizens of society. The fact that citizens increasingly live in pluralist societies makes compelling Rawls' advocacy of a minimal political doctrine that will ensure people's rights and liberties within its society. I agree. Yet, this does not mean that we need to dispel completely any notion of community in order for Rawls' theory to work. In the previous sections, I attempt to show the link between Rawls' notion of social cooperation and that of community. We do not have to have a comprehensive notion of community for us to think of community: community is often defined as a group of people with shared aims or purposes. This fits with Rawls' fair terms of social cooperation, whereby people cooperate in order to set and accept the rules and procedures that govern our conduct for a just society.

In the second instance, Rawls' liberal theory attempts to create a political theory in order to accommodate people's varying conceptions of the good. In so doing, he automatically sets up a particular community that promotes and protects the concept of reasonable pluralism. This is not void of any community, but rather it creates a particular political culture, and some would argue, a particular community. I think it is mistaken to assume that communities require a comprehensive doctrine in order for us to define them as such. We do not necessarily need communities to have strong religious or moral claims in order for people to feel part of a community. We can conceive of community by the shared and common aims of the people in society.

We further see that the fair terms of social cooperation have certain moral values implicit within its framework: that of egalitarian principles. The fair terms of social cooperation are not completely value-neutral, but promote certain dispositions that are conducive toward liberal aims in a just society. The ideals of reciprocity and mutuality hold moral weight. Rawls acknowledges that there is not a sharp distinction between completely neutral doctrines and comprehensive doctrines. Rather, it is a matter of degree (Rawls 1985). Yet distinctive features can be discerned between comprehensive doctrines and his political theory. While the values of liberal theory are based on principles of justice and do carry moral weight, they do not rely upon larger historical, religious and philosophical foundations (Rawls 1995: 133–4). That is not to suggest, however, that every comprehensive doctrine is permissible. Rawls' political theory rests upon 'a willingness to propose fair terms of social cooperation that others as free and equal also might endorse, and to act on these terms, provided others do, even contrary to one's own interest; and second, a recognition of the burdens of judgment' (Rawls 1993: 2–3).

In suggesting this, Rawlsian liberalism could be defined as a community through its a) deliberative aspects toward social cooperation, b) in people's common aim toward developing and maintaining a just society, and c) the implicit moral values based on egalitarianism. This does not mean that all communities underneath this overarching liberal community necessarily need to celebrate these liberal principles within their private spheres of community (within the limits of reasonable pluralism), nor does it necessarily mean that everyone is required to participate in this liberal community. Rather, this first level of the political liberal community sets conditions in which a just society requires individuals to deliberate through the fair terms of social cooperation. Rawls' liberal theory should not veer away from a conception of community within its framework and, moreover, may be considered as a community in this more deliberative light.

Having made this argument, I do want to note an important caveat to this last claim. Not all communities are constitutive of liberal theory. Illiberal communities would not be acceptable within the liberal framework. Further, even reasonable communities that fall within the considerations of justice would not necessarily comply with the constitutive aspect of liberal theory. The specific community in which one could adopt this argument is within the narrow parameters of a shared public political community in which to set the agreed-upon rules and regulations of a just society. So it is not sufficient to say that community is constitutive of liberal theory. The notion of community must be qualified under the terms that I have set out above in adhering to the principles of justice, and those that specifically assist toward the development of reciprocity and mutual respect, as citizens as free and equal persons under a fair system of social cooperation.

Let me sum up thus far. A liberal conception of community can be thought of in the following ways. Individuals may find belonging to or identifying with a community valuable for various reasons. Liberals acknowledge this point and protect individuals' interests within a capacity for a conception of the good, within the limits of reasonable pluralism. Second, social cooperation has implicit and explicit aspects of community. Community may be instrumental in developing dispositions conducive to the ideals of social cooperation. Further, community may be essential to social cooperation: the process by which people come together, which is stronger than the mere presence of people, already implies being a part of community. This leads to the final claim that liberal theory implies a particular political community.

In the next section of the chapter, I want to consider how Rawls reconciles incompatible doctrines, despite initial attempts at agreement through the fair terms of social cooperation as reasonable and rational persons.

Burdens of judgement
Up until this point, Rawls puts great weight on the assumption that people are able to cooperate in a reasonable and rational manner in which to set the accepted rules and regulations for conduct in society. Let's consider, however, that despite individuals' sincere attempts to 'draw inferences, weigh evidence, and balance competing considerations', we arrive at two completely reasonable yet differing and incompatible conclusions (ibid.: 55). The consequence of using the fair system of social cooperation as the process for determining fair and just procedures is that there may still be disagreement among reasonable and rational persons. Rawls attends to this dilemma in what he refers to as 'the burdens of judgement'.

As reasonable and rational persons, we make different kinds of judgements in the deliberative process. Rawls provides a list, which is not exhaustive, that influences our judgements as reasonable and rational persons. Evidence may be complex and difficult to assess. Individuals may give different weight and import to various aspects of the issue, thus arriving at different conclusions. The subject matter for consideration, such as political or moral matters, may rely heavily on judgement and inter-pretation. How we assess and weigh the evidence is shaped by our life experiences, which consequently may cause our judgements to diverge. Normative considerations and differing values on both sides of the debate make it difficult to have one answer or solution (ibid.: 54–8). Rawls suggests that in circumstances whereby individuals have gone through this process, yet arrive at different conclusions, we have to foster toleration under the burdens of judgement within the boundaries of 'reasonable pluralism'. He states:

> The evident consequence of the burdens of judgement is that reasonable persons do not all affirm the same comprehensive doctrine. Moreover, they also recognize that all persons alike, including themselves, are subject to those burdens, and so many reasonable comprehensive doctrines are affirmed, not all of which can be true (indeed none of them may be true). The doctrine any reasonable person affirms is but one reasonable doctrine among others. (Rawls 1993: 60)

What is considered to be reasonable, however, is loosely defined. Rawls has three criteria for determining reasonable doctrines. First, 'a reasonable doctrine is an exercise of theoretical reason: it covers the major religious, philosophical, and moral aspects of human life in a more or less consistent and coherent manner'. Second, 'a reasonable comprehensive doctrine is also an exercise of practical reason'. Third, 'while a reasonable comprehensive view is not necessarily fixed and unchanging, it normally belongs to, or draws upon, a tradition of thought and doctrine' (ibid.: 59). Rawls does not want to evaluate comprehensive moral doctrines as to what is considered 'true' or 'correct'. If he is to be sincere about endorsing diversity and toleration, the political doctrine has to concede and allow unreasonable doctrines within the confines of reasonable pluralism.

Rawls makes a distinction for the allowance of *unreasonable* doctrines within the scope of reasonable pluralism that deserve our respect, from those of *intolerable* doctrines. We accept and assume that there will exist some forms of unreasonable doctrines. We tolerate those unreasonable doctrines in preserving the greater political ideals of diversity and toleration. Yet we constrain comprehensive doctrines that are intolerable: specifically, those that threaten and undermine the essential principles of justice that govern society.

Having said this, liberal theory can and does make judgements about better and worse ways of life and, in so doing, does 'encourage and discourage certain comprehensive doctrines and their associated values' (Rawls 2001: 151). Two criteria are used to discourage particular comprehensive doctrines: 'those that are in direct conflict with the principles of justice, and those that may be admissible but fail to gain adherents under the political and social conditions of a just constitutional regime' (ibid.: 154). So for example, oppression of a person due to their race, gender or ethnicity is subject to certain constraints. Similarly, any group that acquires the control of a state and oppresses others is also unreasonable.

Determining what is considered a reasonable community under Rawls' theory, however, is difficult to assess when we begin to make those sorts of evaluations of what is considered unreasonable and intolerable. Callan (1997) notes that what is to be considered reasonable within a just society brings us to the question: 'How do we conceive the standards that govern public reason in a liberal democracy so as to include all sources of diversity (and only those sources of diversity) that deserve our respect?' (p. 22). Once you ask questions of inclusion, then you have the corresponding notion of exclusion. Deciding which forms of community may be unworthy of respect, by infracting on the basic principles of social justice, already treads on moral ground of what is considered to be 'good' or 'better' over communities that are 'bad' or 'worse'.

To address the dilemma of what constitutes 'reasonable pluralism' as is posed by Callan, I will turn in the final section of this chapter to attempts to clarify various degrees to which communities may fall within reasonable pluralism.

Reasonable pluralism
Community practices within Rawls' liberal theory may be categorized as follows:

1. Communities that assist and support dispositions of reciprocity and equal respect under a fair system of social cooperation as free and equal persons both in the private and public sphere.
2. Communities that may not have dispositions of reciprocity and equal respect in their private association, but concede and

respect the public political process that is built on reciprocity and equal respect as free and equal persons.

3. Communities that do not support dispositions of reciprocity and equal respect in their private sphere, and in which the values or practices may impact negatively to a limited degree on other members in the public sphere who are not members of that community.

4. Communities that do not support dispositions of reciprocity and equal respect in their private sphere, and that *grossly impede* members in the public sphere in ways that are abhorrent to other members in the public sphere and negligent under the considerations of justice.

Within Rawls' notion of reasonable pluralism, the first two categories would be reasonable communities in a liberal pluralist society. The third category might refer to Rawls' unreasonable community in that it infringes on individuals, who are not members of that community, but *may* still be allowable within the limits of toleration for a pluralist society. The fourth category would be 'unreasonable' and 'intolerable' communities and would be constrained within the limits of reasonable pluralism. It is easier to distinguish between the first and second categories, but it is difficult to assess the differences between the third and fourth categories.

Rawls does not provide much assistance in his definition of a reasonable doctrine to make a clear distinction between unreasonable and intolerable communities (Rawls 1993: 59). Most communities could argue that they have a major religious, philosophical or moral doctrine, exercise practical reason and draw upon a tradition of thought. The Nazi regime could arguably have elements of all three categories (Mandle 1999: 93), as would other contentious group practices within the Ku Klux Klan, the Taliban or the Black Panthers. Rawls' loose definition of a reasonable doctrine creates a dilemma for distinguishing between unreasonable and intolerable communities.

I will not spend too much time on the first two types of reasonable communities in a liberal pluralist society. These first two categories are relatively uncontested positions within the boundaries of reasonable pluralism. Rather, I wish to develop the distinction between unreasonable and intolerable communities in greater detail and, in so doing, provide clearer distinctions between the two categories that extend beyond Rawls' weak definition.

In the first category are those communities that promote, assist or extend dispositions of reciprocity and mutual respect in the private and public spheres. Communities may foster the practices that are characteristic of reciprocity and mutual respect within their practices. They may, for instance, foster an appreciation for listening to others, respecting a diversity of opinions, debating the merits of a position and so forth. Debating societies or students' unions are also types of associations that develop specific dispositions, which directly develop dispositions conducive for the public political sphere. Other communities may not necessarily have a specific mandate that fosters public political dispositions, but may extend their private mandate to that of larger public issues. Communities may assist in charitable fund-raising, they may be vocal and supportive of political movements that advance the positions of gender equality, better social welfare programmes for the poor and the like. The mandates of communities are such that they promote and extend public political dispositions in their private associations, which also extend into the public political sphere.

We may still have reasonable communities despite the fact that they do not necessarily support public political dispositions. Communities may be hierarchical or authoritative; they may have practices that do not endorse certain opportunities for particular members within their traditional practices; communities may foster values that are contrary to the aims of reciprocity and mutual respect. The internal practices of that community may be such that they place greater import on the traditional practices and rituals of their community that may conflict with interests in the public political sphere. Assuming that members of a community have the ability to enter or exit that community,[2] these communities may still be considered reasonable if they concede that they should adhere to the basic political conception of free and equal persons in a pluralist society despite the fact that they disagree with these aims within their private sphere. Secret societies that restrict a particular gender or race from entering, traditional religious practices that may curtail the economic opportunities of women and hierarchical groups that give greater status to particular members of a group – all of which may have specific mandates that conflict with the two higher order principles of persons as free and equal – may still be allowable so long as they conform to the public political conception. Rosenblum writes:

Laws do not require the internal life of *every* association to conform to public norms and practices; they do not prohibit racial, religious, or gender discrimination, enforce due process, or impose a democratic structure of authority on every group. We do not favor congregational churches over hierarchic ones, or mandate worker control over other forms of management ... In short, liberal democracy in the United States does not command strict congruence everywhere and 'all the way down'. (Rosenblum 1998: 36)

Liberal societies attempt to restrict their interference in private associations, even if those associations may not promote liberal and democratic values that help to foster a public sphere. A pluralist society acknowledges that various communities are allowed to espouse different norms and values within reason.

In the third category are communities that do not imbue the values of free and equal persons within a fair system of social cooperation at the private sphere, *and* that impinge on non-members to some extent in the public sphere. For instance, groups that have a particular negative bias towards certain members of the public, may not only hold these views within their private group, but may distribute hate literature in the larger public setting. Their intolerant views on a particular group of individuals are not constrained within the private activities of the group, but extend into the public sphere and infringe on others' rights. In some countries, this would be considered unreasonable, yet tolerable in upholding freedom of expression. For instance, in the United States hate literature is permissible, although not necessarily condoned by the state. Similarly, the distribution of pornography in public settings may be seen as a form of violence to women (Rosenblum 1999), yet is still allowable. Yet, in other countries, the infringement of one group's views to the detriment of other persons in the public sphere is both unreasonable and intolerable. In Britain, for instance, the distribution of hate literature is not permissible; and yet pornography is widely distributed and permissible. The interpretation of conflicting rights and what is permissible in the public sphere widely diverges from nation to nation (Dworkin 2002).

Rawls does not provide a clear evaluative marker in this case, and instead remains fairly and purposely ambivalent on the matter (Rawls 1993: 59). One of the consequences of accepting the burdens of judgement is that we do not know what counts as 'true' – be it moral, religious or philosophical differences. Because we do not have decisive ways in which to decide what counts as reasonable and unreasonable, we must have strong grounds to suggest that some communities are intolerable and unacceptable in society. 'Otherwise our account runs the danger of being arbitrary and exclusive' (ibid.: 59). So despite our views that some communities are contrary to the principles of free and equal persons, we may still have to *tolerate* them within the boundaries of reasonable pluralism. 'Views that would suppress altogether the basic rights and liberties affirmed in the political conception, or suppress them in part, say its liberty of conscience, may indeed exist, as there will always be such views' (ibid.: 65). If we are to be sincere in our attempts to allow for contrasting comprehensive doctrines (even those that may be unreasonable), and if we acknowledge that we have to accept the notion of tolerance under the burdens of judgement, then we have to allow a broad enough scope of reasonable and unreasonable communities within reasonable pluralism.

Having said this, Rawls does not believe that 'pluralism' in and of itself, is sufficient: some communities are intolerable in a pluralist society. In attempts to provide a distinction between unreasonable and intolerable comprehensives doctrines, Rawls suggests that only when a comprehensive doctrine poses a 'serious injury to the state' do such views become intolerable. This is a stringent criterion and one that is difficult to demonstrate. They must show that the basic structure is under threat of collapsing, free speech is curtailed, basic liberties are restricted and there is a general suspension of the ways in which the political public sphere operates (ibid.: 355). Rawls points out that in no period of (American) history has such a crisis existed where there was an utter collapse of the basic liberal principles (ibid.: 355).

If we take Rawls' division of the reasonable doctrine as the base criteria for intolerable communities, then many unreasonable communities are permissible within the limits of reasonable pluralism. So long as a particular comprehensive doctrine does not threaten the very existence of the public political system under the fair system of cooperation as free and equal persons, then it seems permissible to allow them, however morally loathsome they may be.

This stance is one that is shared by Rosenblum (1998). Rosenblum contends that what is important is that individuals experience the 'shifting involvements among associations' within the 'experience of pluralism' (p. 17). The process of joining, participating and exiting various associations – belonging to and disassociating from communities – will teach individuals more about living in a pluralist society than the curtailment of morally reprehensible communities. It is better, for instance, for individuals to have some form of association and affiliation than none at all. A paramilitary leader explains extremists as follows:

> Out [he told an interviewer] they're liable to do most anything at any time without anybody knowing it except them. If they decide they want to go out and blow somebody up, okay, they go out and blow somebody up. But if they're part of a group ... well, then there's a good chance someone in the organization will know about it and they're going to take steps to bring this person under control. (Ezekiel 1996: 288, cited in Rosenblum 1998: 272)

Rosenblum contends that, despite the hostile group practices that they may imbue, extremists may benefit from participating in these communities in at least a couple of ways: first, they may provide a lifeline to individuals who are otherwise isolated and alienated and, in this way, may provide a form of attachment and belonging to persons who may otherwise take extreme actions against either themselves or others; second, despite the offensive mandates of paramilitary or hate groups, many such members will eventually find other connections to other associations that have more acceptable norms and practices within a liberal society (ibid.: 272–6). This is an empirical claim that cannot be evaluated here, but it does raise an interesting issue of whether a greater allowance of communities through a notion of toleration may provide unexpected benefits to those individuals and to public society. Rosenblum's view is one that subscribes to a generous scope for toleration of groups in a pluralist society. In turn, a person's shifting involvements in communities will be such that they will not be static or ossified, but rather complex and changing within the general moral climate of a liberal society.

This may be an unpalatable place for many liberals, in the broad acceptance of what is permissible in Rawls' reasonable pluralism. If we are to look only to Rawls' reasonable doctrines for providing an evaluative mechanism, then almost all communities are permissible in a pluralist society. However, this is not the definitive set of criteria by which to evaluate the various comprehensive doctrines within reasonable pluralism. While Rawls' definition of reasonable doctrines offers a wide scope of permissible communities, he does have a stronger conception when he articulates the conditions of the priority of the 'right' over the 'good'.

The priority of the right over the good has a number of aspects, in that it: requires some notion of goodness as rationality; guarantees primary goods; addresses permissible comprehensive doctrines; considers political virtues; and addresses the idea of the good in a well-ordered political society (Rawls 1993: 176). I wish to address the second and third criteria, that of primary rights and permissible comprehensive doctrines, within Rawls' notion of the priority of the right.

The idea of primary rights ensures that, in any political or social organization, people will be accorded basic fundamental rights and protected under considerations of justice. In order to secure the principles of justice, people must be accorded basic primary goods in order to be able to have such capacities. Primary goods include the following:

(a) basic rights and liberties, also given by a list;
(b) freedom of movement and free choice of occupation against a background of diverse opportunities;
(c) powers and prerogatives of offices and positions of responsibility in the political and economic institutions of the basic structure;
(d) income and wealth; and finally
(e) the social bases of self-respect. (ibid.: 181)

This basic list provides the minimum threshold that citizens require to function in the public political sphere. Comprehensive doctrines must acknowledge and concede these primary goods to individuals in order to ensure their status as free and equal persons.

In order to secure a list of primary goods, Rawls introduces the political conception of the person which, combined with the two higher-order interests of liberty and equality, provide the requisite background for protecting individuals' needs and requirements (ibid.: 178). 'An effective political conception of justice includes, then, a political understanding of what is to be publicly recognized as citizen's needs and hence as advantageous for all' (ibid.: 179). The political conception of the person determines what justice requires for persons in the public realm.

At this point, Rawls states that comprehensive doctrines are impermissible in two ways (as opposed to the one way to which he refers under his conception of reasonable doctrines). Recall earlier that Rawls wishes to discourage certain comprehensive doctrines if: 'their associated ways of life may be in direct conflict with the principles of justice; or else they may be admissible but fail to gain adherents under the political and social conditions of a just constitutional regime' (ibid.: 196). The first instance replies to practices within a particular community that do not respect the considerations of justice: for instance, those practices that oppress individuals, such as slavery, a caste system and the like. The second instance is whereby the survival of certain communities conflicts with the very basic structure of society: those that may require the coercing of all other doctrines under their regime, and having total control of power in a society.

How then are we to reconcile between permissible communities within Rawls' weaker conception of reasonable doctrines to the stronger claim of the priority of right over the good within the limits of political liberalism? A helpful distinction can be made between *intolerable communities* and *intolerable conduct in communities*.[3] Intolerable communities may be a state's interference or legal prohibition of a community. Intolerable conduct in communities may be the state's interference with particular practices that may conflict with considerations of justice. The former is a much more invasive procedure in attempts to abolish a particular community but would be rarely imposed, whereas the latter is less invasive in restricting only those practices that are detrimental to the stability of the public political order, but could be more liberally applied by the state.

I contend that Rawls' conception of a reasonable doctrine may be an attempt to address the more invasive policy of a state's power to curtail a particular community. This would make sense of Rawls' reluctance for the state to curtail an actual community unless it could demonstrate 'serious injury to the state'. And, if this is the case, only in very few cases would a liberal state ban a community.

The Irish Republican Army (IRA) is one such organization which the British government has deemed illegal. The justification for the British government is as follows: the IRA's mandate is a military organization whose primary directive is to overthrow the British state in Northern Ireland using any means, violent or otherwise. As has been demonstrated numerous times over the past century, the IRA's mission could arguably be a serious threat to the British state, with assassination attempts on political figures, and terrorist attempts to cause general instability and fear in the

British public sphere. In this circumstance, the British government feels that the aims of the IRA pose a serious threat to the
public political order of the state.

To prohibit an entire community, however, is a very invasive
procedure, and one which liberals, rightly, are very reluctant to
endorse. The priority of the right over the good and the political
conception of the person, however, provide a way in which to
limit certain *practices* within a community that may be intolerable,
without the outright prohibition of a community. Mandle (1999)
suggests that although this is a stronger version of what constitutes
a reasonable comprehensive doctrine, it 'represents a commitment
to the ideal of society as a fair system of cooperation among free
and equal citizens, recognizing the burdens of judgement, and
accepting the duty of civility' (Mandle 1999: 94). In this case, the
liberal ideals of free and equal persons override concerns for
intolerable moral doctrines in a liberal society.

Inhibiting certain practices in community is not to be taken
lightly, and Rawls is cognizant of this. However, such constraints
do not necessarily require that the community itself be abolished;
rather, it suggests that communities may need to reform certain
practices that grossly infringe on an individual. Rawls acknowledges that the result of this is that some communities may die out,
while others thrive. However, 'no society can include within itself
all forms of life. We may indeed lament the limited space, as it
were, of social worlds, and of ours in particular; and we may
regret some of the inevitable effects of our culture and social
structure' (ibid.: 197).

If we interpret Rawls under the stronger claim that comprehensive doctrines must adhere to the considerations of justice, we
have a much stronger evaluative claim. We further see that
intolerable practices in communities within categories three and
four would be constrained under the considerations of justice.
The criteria do not necessarily rest on what is at first glance
morally offensive and objectionable, but whether the practices of a
particular community reject 'the basic essentials of a democratic
regime' (Rawls 1995: 134). This stronger version of a permissible
community now affects not only the practices that a community
may infringe on non-members of a community, but it may well
include members within the community who may be denied the
basic considerations of justice as free and equal persons. The
political conception of the person, thus, has implications for
practices within any comprehensive doctrine.

Communities are not an ossified construction, but are changing and evolving. Communities that are unable or unwilling to change practices that commit direct harm to individuals should be constrained by the principles of justice. Rawls assertively comments, 'if a comprehensive conception of the good is unable to endure in a society securing the familiar equal basic liberties and mutual toleration, there is no way to preserve it consistent with democratic values as expressed by the idea of society as a fair system of cooperation among citizens viewed as free and equal' (1993: 198). Those communities unable or unwilling to change those practices that compromise the principles of liberty and equality are not be protected within the limits of reasonable pluralism.

The distinction between intolerable communities and intolerable conduct in communities is a useful evaluative mechanism for considering what may be permissible within the limits of reasonable pluralism. While liberals are hesitant to ban a community as a whole, liberals may have more ability to constrain particular practices that contravene the principles of liberty and equality. This does not set the evaluative marker particularly high, but does provide a clearer line for constraining certain practices that infringe on individuals as free and equal persons.

The distinctions between reasonable, unreasonable, tolerable and intolerable communities thus provide an important theoretical framework for discerning particular practices in school communities, and schools and their communities that support, are ambivalent, or contravene liberal ideals of free and equal persons.

Liberal communities and the limits within reasonable pluralism

To bring together the elements of this chapter, let me summarize how liberal theory provides a normative conception of community.

1. Communities fall within the constraints of justice. The two higher order principles, liberty and equality, are of primary concern.
2. Liberals value community under individuals' capacity for a conception of the good. They understand that communities can be worthwhile and valuable in people's lives. Recognizing people's diverging interests and needs, liberal theory protects various reasonable communities.

3. There is an implicit notion of community within the terms of social cooperation. The basis for Rawls' theory rests on the assumption that people are cooperating members of a society. I argue that community is instrumental and essential to developing dispositions of reciprocity and mutuality through one's participation in community.
4. Competing comprehensive doctrines are accommodated by the terms set out under the burdens of judgement and the ideal of toleration.
5. Intolerable communities can be curtailed only if they pose a serious threat to the stability of the state. Only in extreme cases can a liberal state ban a community.
6. Intolerable conduct within a community, however, can be held to a stronger conception within the priority of the right, and the political conception of the person.

These broad principles lead us to consider communities in particular ways and with particular ramifications. It provides a theoretical foundation for evaluating communities that are beneficial, tolerated or impermissible in a liberal society.

The next chapter applies the four categories for discerning communities in schools that would be celebrated, tolerated or impermissible within a liberal conception of community.

Notes

1. Callan (1997) challenges Rawls' assertion that his theory is merely a political theory, and not a comprehensive moral doctrine. Callan asserts that Rawls' theory is more comprehensive than Rawls wishes to admit. What counts as 'reasonable' within the limits of political liberalism begins to tread on evaluative statements of what is better and worse, or what are acceptable and unacceptable ways of living. This dividing line of what is to be included as 'reasonable' or as 'unreasonable' pushes Rawls' political liberalism into the grey areas of a moral comprehensive doctrine. Whether Rawls' theory is comprehensive or not cannot be resolved here. However, if I am to build a conception of community within Rawls' framework, I must accept that community must be defined within the constraints of justice.
2. If members do not have the capacity to freely enter and exit the community, it may be contested whether the state has an obligation to protect vulnerable members within that

community. I have already discussed this issue at greater length in Chapter 3 between Kymlicka's (1989) assumption that people must have the ability to enter and exit a community with the concerns that Gutmann (2003) poses regarding vulnerable members and the obstacles that they face in leaving a community.

3. I would like to thank Eamonn Callan for helping me to clarify and develop this distinction.

CHAPTER 6

Permissible Communities in Liberal Education

Having laid a necessary theoretical foundation in the previous chapter, I return to the primary task of how to distinguish communities that are important to foster in schools from those that are less desirable. The theoretical framework that I have set out provides an evaluative mechanism for school communities, and schools and their communities. Whether the community is part of the particular ethos of a school or whether external community practices influence school policy and practice, the principles set within reasonable pluralism provide a way in which to distinguish between permissible and impermissible community practices. We apply the categories set within reasonable pluralism to see which communities foster and develop liberal principles; communities that may disagree with liberal principles in the private sphere, but concede their importance in the public sphere, and communities that contravene liberal principles both in private and public spheres. Recall that category four collapses into category three, when we use the stronger indicator of constraining intolerable conduct both within and external to communities.

To illustrate how this evaluative framework can be applied to schools, I consider three school communities that parallel the categories developed under reasonable pluralism. The first case illustrates a school that furthers liberal ideals within the ethos of the school and through greater links to the community. Such a school promotes liberal ideals both in private school activities and in civic affairs among the greater public. The second case considers Muslim faith communities' attempt to reconcile their private religious views with the provisions mandated in liberal state schools. The final case examines a Christian fundamentalist school whose explicit mandate is to teach the values of its own faith community to the exclusion of other views. These three case studies help to elucidate key issues that arise when considering the permissibility of various communities in schools, and the degree to which liberal ideals can accommodate various values that communities wish to promote in their children's learning in schools.

I have put these educational examples in three separate sections in order to make explicit the general characteristics of communities within the boundaries of reasonable pluralism. My aim is not necessarily to decide whether the specific cases that I use should be permitted or constrained. Rather, my aim is to illustrate how liberal principles can be applied to develop school policy more generally regarding the provision of various communities. I wish to draw particular attention to those community practices that fall within and beyond acceptable boundaries for schooling from a liberal perspective. What remains of paramount importance for liberals is that 'children have a substantive opportunity to become autonomous adults; on the liberal view this principle has very high priority in evaluating education policy, outweighing, for example, any parental interest in having a child educated at a school which promotes the parents' religion' (Brighouse 2002b).

The liberal values promoted at the Anglo-European School cause little concern for liberals. I will not devote much time to this school, as it does not raise particular concerns for liberals other than to illustrate community practices that fall within the acceptable liberal boundaries. The example of the Christian fundamentalist school illustrates a stark contrast to the first case in its expressed and intentional repression of liberal values. This is a clear example where liberals would find the practices of this school community unacceptable within the boundaries of reasonable pluralism. It is the second case, that of Muslim communities, that proves to be a difficult and grey area within a liberal conception of community. Communities that are willing to deliberate within the fair terms of social cooperation indicate a *prima facie* reasonableness as is developed in liberal theory. It is for this reason that a greater proportion of this chapter is devoted to the second case, where finding an agreeable compromise between liberal educators and Muslims is more challenging than in the first and third cases.

The Anglo-European School

The first case that I draw upon is a school located in Ingatestone, Essex, which fosters students' appreciation of their own identity and that of others through a particular global citizenship ethos. Through a whole-school approach, the Anglo-European School exemplifies liberal ideals through community-oriented practices both within and beyond school walls (Potter 2002: 160). The aims of the Anglo-European School are:

- To provide the highest quality of education that is enriched by a strong European and international dimension.
- To respect individuals and their culture while developing an understanding of and a respect for the culture of others.
- To give students the academic and social skills which enable them to move freely and productively beyond the boundaries of their own community. (Anglo-European School 2003)

These aims are explicitly reflective of liberal ideals. The first aim provides an overarching principle that pupils are to have a quality of education that will be of a high standard both at the local and international level. The second aim emphasizes respect for oneself and others. The third aim places importance on facilitating pupils' present and future opportunities by developing skills that will enable them to move 'freely' and 'beyond the bounds of their own community'. Each of these aims is conducive to and exemplifies values welcomed in a liberal education.

Implementation of these aims is reflected at multiple levels of the school, both in its cross-curricular approach and the overall ethos of the school. Two key curricular objectives emphasize the importance of learning about one's own and others' cultures. One key curricular objective is that all students learn a foreign language. The rationale is twofold. First, students who learn a foreign language have greater present and future access to communities not of their own language. Second, learning a second language provides greater access to that language's history and culture, thus broadening perspectives.

The second curricular objective develops a strong international perspective through a number of initiatives. The Anglo-European School has established 14 Partner Schools across Europe, and one in India. Visits and exchange programmes are provided at various years at the school. Further, the school has numerous citizenship and international aid projects with larger international organizations. They include: Amnesty International, AIDS Awareness,

Landmine Action, United Nations Association, WorldWatch, UNICEF and UNA.[1] All sixth-form students participate in the Creative, Action and Service (CAS) programme as a component of the citizenship education. Further, all sixth-form students are involved in international study and visits programmes.

To encourage students' participation and appreciation of this European dimension within their school life, the Anglo-European School has created a European citizenship award. The award fosters:

- knowledge and understanding of Europe, its peoples and its place in the world;
- positive but critical attitudes towards other peoples and cultures;
- respect for different ways of life, beliefs, opinions and ideas;
- language capability to facilitate communication and cooperation;
- skills for economic life. (Potter 2002: 162–3)

The international and open perspective of the school crosses curricular boundaries, and expands to broader activities in and beyond the school.

This school is demonstrative of policies and practices that are conducive to broader liberal ideals in society. Emphasis is placed on respect and mutuality across cultures, both at a local and global level. Students are actively encouraged to learn about other cultures through their participation in language courses, exchange programmes, and citizenship projects. Open communication and understanding among pupils and staff are transmitted in their tangible policies and practices. The Anglo-European School is an example of developing an ethos that fosters liberal aims.

Muslim faith communities and liberal education

This section examines the second category that I defined within the boundaries of reasonable pluralism: specifically, faith communities that espouse particular traditional roles within the community and yet acknowledge broader liberal values in society. In particular, I consider Muslim communities in the United Kingdom and their attempts to pass on the values and faith to their children, yet balance this with their intention to integrate their children socially as British citizens. I will argue that the Muslims' attempts to expose their children to liberal education while attempting to retain their faith within the private community are reasonable within a pluralist society. Similarly, so long as children are taught fundamental liberal education aims that develop their capacities as autonomous individuals, then it is also reasonable to allow certain concessions to communities in schools in respecting their faith. The concessions allowable in schooling are dependent on the criticalness of the particular learning objective towards their capacity to be free and equal persons.

Muslim communities in England comprise the third largest religious group in the United Kingdom, only behind Anglican and Roman Catholic faiths (Halstead 1986: 3). It is a hetero-geneous faith community, comprising various sects underneath the umbrella of Islamic faith. This is not unique to Islamic faith, but is indicative of religion more generally. Defining the one 'true' faith among Christianity, Judaism and Islam would mis-represent the heterogeneity of the various strands within each of these faith communities. My intent is to pull out particular con-troversies within various sects of the Muslim community, recognizing that this is not a complete picture of the Islamic faith.

Muslim faith communities in the UK are particularly contentious, as compared to Christian faiths in UK. Unlike the distinct separation between church and state in the United States, that is not the case in the UK. Roman Catholic and Church of England schools are a prominent feature throughout the UK. The difficulty with providing concessions to the Islamic faith, and particularly with the present debate regarding state funding grants for Muslim voluntary schools, is the perception that the Islamic faith will inhibit girls' opportunities as autonomous individuals. Understanding the present political situation in UK with regard to Muslim communities and faith-based schools helps to locate this debate within the larger theoretical debate that I wish to develop.

Although Muslims recognize the importance for boys and girls to be educated, they see different established roles between them. Girls are taught to value the importance of their role as 'wife, mother and manager of the home', while boys are taught the 'role as provider' (Halstead 1993: 61). These roles are not seen as hierarchical between men and women, but rather are advocated as complementary to the relationship between husband and wife in Muslim society.

Further, certain practices within the faith fall within the ambit of traditional communities. For instance, girls and boys are not allowed to intermingle outside the extended family once they reach puberty. For Muslims, adolescence is a period in life where girls and boys are particular vulnerable, and one in which proper guidance from the family is essential to their development. Risk of any exposure to sexual relationships, ranging from sexual harassment to premarital relations, could bring shame to the child and dishonour for that family. It is common for Muslims to arrange marriages, where a careful selection process is made, checking to see that a proper match is made based on backgrounds, economic status and interests.

It is thus understandable that some educational practices found in secular and Christian schools may be offensive to Muslim families. Wearing required gym attire comprising shorts or, similarly, participating in swimming lessons – both of which bare their legs – may be offensive to the Islamic faith (Halstead 1994a). Similarly, being required to fulfil the dance component of a physical education programme by dancing with the opposite sex is also forbidden (ibid.: 314). Participating in music lessons may also contravene principles within this faith (Halstead 1994b). Finally, attending a co-education school in secondary schools is a contentious problem among Muslims due to their strict adherence to not allowing intermingling between the sexes (Halstead 1993, 1994a).

Halstead suggests that many Muslim parents have two main educational goals for their children:

1. the preservation, maintenance and transmission of their distinctive beliefs and values, both through direct teaching and (ideally) through a school ethos informed by these values;
2. access to the opportunities offered by a general education, including living as full British citizens without fear of racism or other forms of prejudice, competing in the employment market on an equal footing with non-Muslims and, more generally, enjoying the benefits of modern scientific and technological progress. (Halstead 1994: 320)

These two educational aims, however, pull in different directions. While Muslims wish to preserve, maintain and transmit their distinctive beliefs to their children, a liberal education exposes a child to multiple ways of viewing the world, and being able to make judgements about one's life. Despite these seemingly irreconcilable differences between the Islamic faith and liberal education, Muslim parents acknowledge that their children should be exposed to the wider society, in which they will live as citizens.

Their willingness to have their children attend state education is an acknowledgement of this.

While Muslim communities recognize the relevance for their children to attend school, they do wish to put certain constraints on the type of schooling their children receive. The difficult task lies in deciding which constraints will or will not compromise the aims of a liberal education. Again, we look to the overarching principles of liberty and equality to assess whether certain educational exemptions will compromise the child's capacity to become autonomous persons. Egalitarian education should promote 'the interest in becoming an autonomous adult; and the interest in equal opportunity' (Brighouse 2000a: 65). If we accept the first principle as part of the role of education, then schools need to consider how best to provide various opportunities and experiences that enhance and expose children to different ways of living. This involves discerning and critically reflecting upon their present way of living, and potentially considering alternative ways of living that may be to their benefit. I am mindful that the development of autonomy is not simply about ensuring one's ability to choose (although there is an element of this). More importantly, it is the ability of individuals to make informed judgements. Exposure to and participation in varied experiences and alternative ways of living help to secure individuals' capacities to lead a life of their own will as adults.

If we agree with Brighouse's position that the role of education is to facilitate children's capacity to become 'autonomous adults' and to enjoy 'equal opportunity', these become the benchmarks for deciding which concessions educators are able to allow. It is a tenuous balance as I have noted in the previous chapter. On the one hand, liberals hope to be sensitive to the multiplicity of values and beliefs within a pluralist society. If this is the case, then a liberal education should reflect this in trying to accommodate various values where possible, even if they may not support liberal ideals. On the other hand, liberals see the pivotal role education provides in a person's present and future opportunities as an autonomous person. And, while access to education is a necessary criterion for the development of autonomous persons, the *type* of education one receives is equally important. A child who is restricted in her learning will be compromised in present and future opportunities.

This dilemma presents itself in balancing Muslim religious beliefs with that of a liberal education. Will certain concessions to

Muslim communities compromise those children's capacity to make informed judgements about their life as a result of certain constraints on their schooling? Let me be clear that the question is not whether Muslim communities are unreasonable, but whether their requests for differential treatment in schools are unreasonable. As I mentioned above, major issues for Muslim communities and provisions for differential treatment in schools include: exemptions from the designated school gym uniforms of shorts; exemptions from dance, music or swimming lessons; and single-sex schools.

Islamic dress codes and state school uniform policies

The first issue addresses the policy of state uniforms that may conflict with established practices in the Islamic faith. From the school's viewpoint, there may be a concern about students wearing suitable clothing that is safe and appropriate for a gym class. They may further wish to have a set uniform in order to constrain the number of requests they receive from various students wishing to deviate from the standard uniform: allowing for one group to be exempt from the uniform may set a precedent for other students who do not like it. The school policy may reflect these positions in trying to have an established and approved gym uniform.

For Muslims, however, the set gym attire of shorts is a significant challenge to their belief that one should not bare one's skin to other persons. As part of the sacred belief of the person, and the constrained choices about sexual relations, showing one's skin is a significant sexual affront to their belief system. While the Islamic faith may have significant dress restrictions placed on the child, the child is still allowed to participate in gym class. The differential treatment refers specifically to clothing, and not to the actual participation in physical education.

It is fairly apparent then that the burden that the gym attire places on the Muslim faith is significant. Conversely, altering the gym attire to accommodate the Muslim community does not necessarily jeopardize the aims of teaching physical education. The request by the Muslims is reasonable in so far as they wish their children to be involved in physical education. If we look back to the two criteria of autonomy facilitation – that of 'autonomous adults' and 'equal opportunity' – the request to alter the required gym attire does not interfere with either principle. Muslim children can still participate in physical education so long as they are not baring skin. Similarly, liberals can easily accommodate this request without compromising the aims of a liberal education.

The issue of Islamic dress has played itself out in different contexts recently. In March 2005, a Muslim girl won a case with England's Appeal Court judges to wear the *jilbab* (a full-length gown that only bares her hands and face) to a school in Luton. The Appeal Court defended her appeal on the grounds of her right to freedom of religion. Shabina Begum was aged 16 at the time of the case. Shabina had previously worn the approved school regulation uniform for Muslims of the *shalwar kameez* (trousers and tunic). In September 2002, however, she informed school authorities that she wished to wear the full *jilbab*. In this case, Shabina was not coerced by her parents to wear the *jilbab* – both her parents were deceased at the time of the case. The Appeal Court felt that it was the duty of the school to show that the school uniform policy could override the right for Shabina to wear her religious dress, which in the eyes of the judges, it could not do.

However, in France, legislation to ban all conspicuous religious symbols has been put in place in the hopes of preserving *laïcité*, separation of church and state, and its hope to preserve equal citizenship for all persons within the confines of public institutions. While the legislation has passed, albeit with protests from various religious communities across the country, it is questionable whether, normatively, the French state is justifed in upholding such a ban.[2]

If we consider the issue of Islamic dress in the context of schooling, the issue centres on whether religious symbols or dress will inhibit that person's capacity to develop or exercise decisions about how they wish to lead their life. In all three cases – that of the gym attire, wearing the *jilbab* to a Luton school and wearing the *hijab* in French schools – the Islamic dress does not *prima facie* restrict the students' access to a liberal education. The parents have not excluded them from state schools, nor have they restricted their children from part of the curriculum. It is difficult to suggest that by wearing a particular aspect of Islamic dress, the children have been compromised in their ability to become autonomous individuals. They are still exposed to the culture of the school and they still learn the subject material of the compulsory curriculum. To ban religious symbols or clothing seems to go beyond the defined criteria as an intolerable practice of a community. And, further, by not accommodating the values of this religious community, we potentially force families away from state schools and mainstream society.

Islamic exemptions for core compulsory courses in the National Curriculum

Restricting students from learning particular lessons in a school requires more deliberation as to the exemption that is being requested. Whereas the policy to amend a particular school policy that does not alter the learning objective is arguably less significant, exemptions from learning a particular objective are more significant. In this case, we must balance the learning objective and its relevance in liberal education to the burdens it may place on the religious community. Participation in music education is one such dilemma that arises in Muslim communities.

Music education is a core subject of the National Curriculum. Music provides a unique form of communication that fosters 'personal expression, reflection and emotional development' (QCA 2003a). Through music, we hope to develop children's ability to listen and to appreciate a variety of music forms. Music also has instrumental benefits that are beneficial to other forms of learning (Temmerman 1991). For instance, music has a strong correlation to mathematics when children learn about rhythm, time signatures and the nature of instruments and their corresponding tonal increments. Verse and rhyme scheme complement the teaching of poetry and English. The process of playing an instrument develops coordination and physical development. Finally, understanding music is a key way in which to understand contemporary society. As an expressive art form, music provides a cultural context in which to describe and criticize society. It is arguable that not to be exposed to music would limit a person's understanding of the society of which she is a part (Hirsch 1988). These arguments lend themselves toward the view that exposure to music is a key component in becoming an autonomous person.

For devout Muslims, however, music is not permissible in Islam (Halstead 1994b). For them, music diverts the individual away from the righteous path of Allah, and contributes to the vices of immorality and sexual promiscuity. Those who believe that the pursuit of music is seen as something that misleads individuals from the path of God cite the following passage:

> And there are among men those who purchase idle talk in
> order to mislead others without knowledge from the path of
> Allah and who throw ridicule upon it; for such there will be
> a humiliating punishment. (Sura 31, v. 6 as cited in Halstead
> 1994b)

To the outsider, this seems at odds with the Muslim faith and their
perceived use of music. Music is used to call people to prayer:
prayer is not spoken, but sung, and drums are a common
instrument in the Islamic faith. Yet, to the devout Muslim, this is
not music but something different that identifies the specific tonal
and rhythmic nuances of the Muslim culture. They regard their
prayers as incantations, not music. Similarly, playing instruments
for pleasure is forbidden while the accompaniment of drumbeats
to their prayers is a key component to their daily ritual. Their
nuanced perceptions of voice and rhythm are entwined with the
specific purposes of their Islamic faith, and one that is not seen as
'music' in and of itself, but serving a greater purpose.

However, Muslims are not unified on their view of music. For
some, music is an integral part of human life. Muslim pop groups
and aspects of Muslim music occur within their faith system.
Muslims who accept music as part of their life quote the passage
from the Qur'an:

> Say, who has forbidden the beautiful gifts from Allah which
> he has provided for his creatures? (Sura 7, v. 32 as cited in
> Halstead 1994)

This view allows and acknowledges the beauty that music provides from their God. It is something not to be ashamed of, but
rather embraced and celebrated.

Most Muslims will agree that music is forbidden if it contains
sexual connotations, be it explicit lyrics or songs that are per-
formed in a suggestive manner. Similarly, they do not condone
music that promotes any activity that is specifically prohibited
among Muslims such as mixed dancing, even if the actual song
does not explicitly promote the activity. Finally, Muslims do not
allow songs that promote a specific religion that is in conflict with
the Qur'an. Religious hymns and other songs of devotion that are
condemned by Islam are unacceptable forms of music.

Given the diverse attitudes toward music by Muslims and their
general reservations about certain types of music, it may be argued
that Muslims should have the ability to withdraw their children,

either partially or entirely, from music. Unlike literacy and numeracy – where it is undisputed that these subjects are essential to autonomous persons – music need not be considered an essential core subject that children must learn. Arguably, many a child has an impoverished or mediocre musical upbringing, and can still sufficiently operate as an individual in society. Music may be seen as frivolous, when formal school time could be devoted to other subjects. This argument is adopted, not only by some members of the Muslim community, but is often put forward by 'Back to Basics' movements, which emphasize a curriculum primarily focused on key curricular objectives such as reading, writing and arithmetic.

Similarly, unlike literacy and numeracy where children require formal training, children may have some exposure to music just by living in a particular society. While the parents' wish may be to minimize their children's exposure to music, it is an endeavour that is bound to fail. People are exposed to music in their daily life, in the media and pervasively throughout public life. Educators perhaps need not worry that children will lack any music appreciation if they are not taught specifically in schools. The liberal demand to ensure that children will have exposure to music can safely be assured by their daily interactions in public life in society. Music might be deemed 'desirable' but not essential to include in schooling.

Children's exposure to music in society might suggest allowing Muslim children to be exempt from music. This argument needs to be tempered with the perceived benefits that a child may derive from attending music. Both intrinsic and instrumental benefits are included in the case for learning music. Intrinsic reasons may include the pleasure an individual may achieve by being exposed to music. In its most basic form, music may bring joy into people's lives. Music is further seen as a powerful medium in which to express views, opinions, passions and, more broadly, the human condition. Exclusion of music limits one powerful way for individuals to express themselves through this medium. While Muslim children will have some exposure to music in their daily living in a liberal society, this raises the question of whether they will acquire an appreciation and understanding of music that may be conducive to their development as autonomous persons. Inadvertent exposure to music may be a basic minimum threshold that all individuals cannot avoid, but formal training ensures that children will have some capacity to enjoy and pursue opportunities that are available in music. The intrinsic benefits children receive and the instrumental benefits that can be derived make a compelling case for its mandated core status in education. If we agree that a) music provides intrinsic and instrumental benefits to children, b) these intrinsic and instrumental benefits contribute to one's autonomy and c) understanding and appreciating music requires more than just inadvertent exposure, then allowing Muslim children to opt out of music education completely is one that would compromise their development as children.

Given these positions, liberals would have difficulty with agreeing to a complete exemption from music education. Schools play a pivotal role in providing opportunities to children that will help to develop them as autonomous individuals, especially in circumstances in which children may have limited opportunities to do so in their local communities (Raz 1986). This does not mean, however, that schools should be insensitive to the Muslim faith and Muslims' specific concerns about music. For example, it is reasonable for schools to be sensitive to the cultural needs by omitting songs that are of a religious nature or that are implicitly or explicitly sexually suggestive.[3]

Islamic provisions for single-sex schools

The final aspect of contention that I wish to draw upon from Muslim communities and their tensions with state schooling is that of single-sex schools. As I mentioned above, Muslims believe that adolescents of different sexes should not intermingle. They wish to avoid the potential sexual harassment that girls may receive during secondary schooling. They are concerned about sexual promiscuousness among teenagers. And finally, they see girls and boys as having distinct and particularly defined gender roles. The concern is so pervasive among Muslim parents that, if they cannot find a single-sex school for their teenage girls, they are often tempted to send them back to their countries of origin during this period of their life (Halstead 1993).

Single-sex schools are not a new phenomenon to the United Kingdom. Both within independent and state schooling, single-sex schools have played a role in independent schools, grammar schools and, to some extent, comprehensive schools. Arguments have been posed on both sides for and against single-sex schools with particular emphasis towards adolescent girls' achievement, and issues of equality of opportunity.

First, single-sex schools may provide greater attention to and better conditions for female students. Female students may be free from male harassment and other forms of male domination that are prevalent in a co-educational school. In mixed schools, boys tend to receive proportionately more attention from teachers than girls, in terms of discipline and attention in class discussions (Halstead 1991). Single-sex schools may offer girls a learning environment without being distracted, embarrassed or intimidated by the opposite sex.

Second, single-sex schools may celebrate the achievements of women, highlighting successful female role models for adolescent girls. For instance, Burgess (1990) points out that males have generally been in senior levels of authority in mixed schooling, providing fewer female role models. Further, textbooks and literature may focus less on the achievements of women in mixed schooling as compared to single-sex schools. Single-sex schools could provide more female role models for girls, and could focus on female role models in society, which may be underemphasized in current mixed schools.

Third, perceived stereotypes about girls' poor achievement in maths and sciences may create a compelling argument for single-sex schools, which provide additional educational support in those subject areas where adolescent girls have traditionally been struggling. However, despite initial higher test scores in single-sex schools, a three-year study examining student achievement in single-sex schools suggests that social class, ability and the tradition of the school is more indicative of higher student achievement, than the actual separation of girls in a single-sex school (Gipps and Elwood 1999). In this study, they suggest that the higher test results in single-sex schools as compared to co-ed schools is indicative of the general trend of girls performing better than boys at the secondary level. One study suggested that single-sex schools tended to attract girls who had higher mean prior achievement, higher social-status backgrounds and more often being from the European or Asian ethnic groups than in co-educational settings (Harker 2000). Accounting for these differences in student enrolment, girls' achievement results were comparable to girls in co-educational schools at the end of sixth form. Student achievement does not appear to be substantially higher in single-sex schools because of the 'single-sex' factor.

Yet, single-sex schools do raise a number of concerns related to fair equality of opportunity (Halstead 1991, Haw 1994). First, girls may not learn the requisite skills to negotiate their place as women alongside men in the workforce – it is simply not a reflection of the 'real world'. Second, a co-education experience may increase girls' ability to learn how to cope in the larger society as adults through a friendly rivalry or competition between boys and girls in a mixed school. Third, while Muslims may wish to protect their daughters from sexual harassment, attending a co-educational school may actually develop their skills to learn how to understand boys in a healthy relationship and, if necessary, to contend with sexual advances of which they do not approve. Removing them from mixed schooling will not eliminate girls' exposure to boys outside school. Finally, arguably the main concern is that single-sex schools may exacerbate the patriarchal divisions that are encouraged by particular faith communities such as the Muslim community. If Muslims see girls and boys as having distinct and particular social roles in society, the potential for girls to be restricted to a single-sex school fosters those dispositions both through formal and informal practices, which may limit their capacity to become autonomous individuals.

In considering positive and negative aspects of single-sex schools, the liberal argument is primarily concerned with facilitating a child's autonomy and ensuring fair equality of opportunity. Determining whether single-sex schools provide fair equality of opportunity through informal and formal practices is more difficult. In one sense, single-sex schools may provide special attention to girls in developing their self-esteem and confidence within a gender-specific education. This may provide benefits to girls in raising their ambitions. On the other hand, they may replicate hierarchical patriarchal patterns that inhibit girls' opportunities within their faith community. It becomes apparent that no conclusive judgements can be made as to whether single-sex schools impede or foster fair equality of opportunity.

Given this dilemma, the burdens of judgement suggest that, when we have deliberated consciously and rigorously and still end up in disagreement, we must accept the differing positions within the burdens of judgement. Unless we can show that single-sex schools hamper girls' fair equality of opportunity, and in this way directly conflict with liberal aims, then we cannot abolish them under the terms of reasonable pluralism. It is insufficient to argue against single-sex schools because they may have the *potential* to inhibit girls' fair equality of opportunity. If this were the case, then many practices in mixed schooling could receive similar objections given the current non-ideal circumstances for girls. This does not suggest, however, that states have no role in regulating single-sex schools. As far as possible, the state can protect girls' interests by monitoring practices in schools so as to facilitate their autonomy and equality of opportunity.

Islamic faith, liberal aims and the fair terms of social cooperation

Muslims have been reasonable in that they recognize the need for their children to be part of larger society. While tensions remain between Islamic faith communities and liberal traditions found in education, they attempt to find a compromise that allows their children to have a general education and still respect their faith. Conversely, in the spirit of tolerance and respect, schools have a reciprocal duty to be sensitive to the values of the Muslim community in so far as they can without jeopardizing liberal aims. Through an open process of deliberation between the two perspectives, that of state schools and Muslim communities, it is usually possible to come to accepted rules and regulations that are acceptable to and respectful of both perspectives.

Bethany Baptist Academy

In this final section of the chapter, I wish to consider communities that do not espouse liberal ideals within their community and, further, do not wish to expose their children to liberal aims. I examine a Christian fundamentalist independent school where children are taught the specific ideals of their faith, and are not exposed to any alternative ways of thinking or living. I argue that in cases where children are not exposed to alternative ways of living, it is justified for the state to interfere with the child's education to ensure principles of liberty and equality.

To articulate intolerable practices of a faith community and their corresponding running of an independent school, I highlight a Baptist Christian fundamentalist school located in the United States. The principal of the school specifically defines Christian as 'all men [*sic*] are born once of the flesh; if they accept Jesus Christ as their personal savior, they are born once again, but the second time as new men in him' (Peshkin 1986: 1). This distinction is the basic definition for Christian fundamentalists in the United States, and one that distinguishes them from other religious communities and their parochial schools. I will highlight the main doctrine at Bethany Baptist Academy (Peshkin 1986) to illustrate a growing movement of similar Christian fundamentalist independent schools across the United States.

Bethany Baptist Academy caters to the Christian fundamentalist community in Illinois. Concerned about children's exposure to secular and alternative worldviews prevalent in public schools, Bethany Baptist Academy was created to insulate and protect their children from the external influences found in other schools. The school doctrine is encompassing in that the school and church are thought of as one – something that is strongly resisted in American politics in their separation of church and state. Students of the school are to reflect and practise the moral religious code both at school and in their private lives. This means that students are expected to attend church, which is located on the school premises, three times a week. The moral code is to be enforced at all times: students who are caught not reflecting the Christian way during school hours and off-hours are to be disciplined and reprimanded for the error of their ways.

The primary educational goal of the school is to abide by the absolute 'Truth' based on literal interpretations of the Christian bible. The Truth to which they ascribe is unquestioning, absolute and universal. Truth is synonymous with God and, as such, has no room for relativity or relativism.[4] Students are shielded from critical scrutiny, and are shielded from other persons who do not share their belief (ibid.: 44). The school does not encourage students to interact with others who hold alternative views; quite the opposite, students – like 'warriors' – are to guard themselves and forcibly resist any form of integration with individuals not of their faith. The school believes that reflection and questioning are to be constrained, while understanding will come from strict obedience to God, and through the guidance and authority that the teachers provide. The classroom reflects this belief, where questioning and deliberation are not to be encouraged; rather, an authoritarian regime is to be maintained in order to discipline students in protecting their vulnerability (ibid.: 47). Dress code and personal grooming reflective of a good Christian is strictly enforced, with the head inspecting student attire and hairstyles. It is the hope that students will aspire to become at minimum *'full-time Christians'* or, ideally, 'dedicate their lives to *full-time Christian service'* (ibid.: 47). A summation of the doctrine by which this Christian fundamental school abides (and similar schools within the American Association of Christian Schools) is based on these key principles:

1. to bring children to salvation;
2. to inform children about the Word of God;
3. to keep children immersed in the Word of God;
4. to keep children separate from the world;
5. to encourage children to proselytize the unsaved;
6. to lead children to enter full-time Christian service as preachers, teachers, evangelists, etc.; and,
7. failing this, to have children become full-time Christians, living their lives, whatever they do, wherever they are, always for the glory of God. (ibid.: 259)

It is unashamedly explicit on creating a 'closed system within the biblical framework' to protect and be servile to 'one doctrine, one truth, and one way' (ibid.: 59; ibid.: 44).

As Bethany Baptist Academy is an independent private school, the school is not required by law to follow any regulated educational standards. Highest priority is given to religious instruction, with English taking second priority (ibid.: 56). All students are required to take a one-year compulsory speech class, as it is seen as a vehicle for speaking and hearing the word of God.[5] Music is placed high on the list of important subjects, as a way to connect to God spiritually (ibid.: 57). While mathematics, social studies and science are taught, they are considered of secondary importance, since they are not fundamental subjects for Christians, and the Christian way of life (ibid.: 57). Teachers have considerable latitude in what they teach, and what they exclude. Books that refer to evolution, secularism and other characteristics unbecoming of a Christian are removed (ibid.: 262–3).

While the intent of state schooling is to prepare students to live in a pluralist society, the Christian fundamentalist school explicitly challenges those assumptions and the premises underlying autonomy. The totalizing aspect of the Christian way of life transmitted in the education of these children is one that is highly problematic and troubling for liberal educators. The self-professed insularity[6] of the Christian fundamentalist school is troubling for a number of reasons. Students are segregated from other children who are not of their faith. The school has no interest in accepting children who are not 'true believers'. The school policy is to protect and separate their children from all other external influences that are not of their faith. This level of insularity is attempted at all levels including censorship of texts, homogeneous grouping of student and staff, and moral codes that influence the child both during and after school. The school specifically enforces obedience and subservience to God, and constrains and inhibits most forms of critical scrutiny. In sum, Bethany Baptist Academy narrowingly constrains the child's opportunities to that of the Christian way both in school, and in wider society. It is clear that this school has no intention of providing opportunities to the child that is not part of the Christian way of life (as is defined within the parameters of Christian fundamentalism). The child is shaped for a particular way of life to which there is little other option. Exposure to other ways of thinking or living is unacceptable and shunned by the school. Students are made to feel shame or guilt should they veer from the path of righteousness. Exiting the community is emotionally and physically difficult.

It is obvious that the aims of Bethany Baptist Academy run counter to that of autonomy-facilitation. Unlike the Anglo-European School that has explicit liberal aims, and the Muslim community's attempts to reconcile tensions between their faith and state schools, Bethany Baptist Academy explicitly rejects liberal aims. Given the expressed and intentional illiberal aims of Bethany Baptist Academy, liberals could proceed in three ways: one option is to accommodate the rights of parents to raise their children in totalizing or all-encompassing communities within the boundaries of toleration; another is to restrain certain practices in a way that the state deems vital in protecting individuals' liberty and equality; a third is to prohibit the entire educational institution that contravenes liberal principles.

If we agree to the first option of allowing parents exclusive rights in educating their child, then we automatically forfeit the possibility of ensuring autonomy-facilitation education, and the broader protections as free and equal persons. I have already argued that this is an unacceptable position to take within the boundaries of reasonable pluralism. Liberty and equality provide the requisite background for ensuring individuals' needs and interests. In ensuring these basic principles, children require a quality of education that will facilitate these capacities. To allow parents such complete freedom, however, to limit the type of education their child receives, could seriously compromise a child's present and future opportunities as a free and equal person. Since Bethany Baptist Academy overtly tries to suppress alternative perspectives, this directly contravenes the basic principles underlying liberty and equality. It is apparent that, if we are to facilitate children's capacities to make informed judgements about how they wish to live, providing alternative perspectives is a critical component. As such, this option is not viable from a liberal perspective. The boundaries of toleration cannot accommodate the extreme perspective of the Christian fundamentalist school.

The radically different option would be to completely ban such a school from existing. If the principles of the school do not reflect the liberal aims of society, then it is conceivable that the state could be justified in the closure of such a school. Not only does the school not reflect the values of greater society, but also actively teaches students to resist and segregate themselves from those who do not support their faith. This aggressive stance may provide the state with enough justification for its closure. Yet again, if we follow the principles set out within reasonable pluralism, we see that such an invasive move by the state should be carried out only if the actions pose a 'serious injury to the state' (Rawls 1993). It is obvious that the teaching of Bethany Baptist Academy, while narrowly focused and illiberal, does not pose a serious threat to the stability of the state. Shutting the school down is not an option within the principles of reasonable pluralism.

If we do not agree to full parental discretion, nor do we agree to the suppression of the illiberal aims of Bethany Baptist Academy, we are left with the second option. Faith communities may run their own educational institution, but must adhere to certain educational standards that will foster a child's future opportunities as an autonomous person. At minimum, the state would be well within its mandate to set regulations that require a core curriculum to be taught to students, which would include a range of perspectives. It would also include developing particular dispositions that enable an individual the capacity to be an autonomous person, such as allowing for debate, critical discussion and open reflection about one's own view and those of others. This does not mean that education must persuade them away from their faith community, but it does require that children be exposed to different ways of living.

State interference would occur against only those practices that are unacceptable within the school community, and not necessarily on the entire institution. This level of interference, however, may be unacceptable for those communities who wish to protect their children from such exposure (Burtonwood 2003). Finding a compromise that is acceptable between the liberal perspective and stronger versions of faith schools is unlikely. As the principal of the school stated:

> If they [state government] passed laws and said they'd forbid
> Christian schools from operating until they were accredited
> by the state standard of accreditation for public schools,
> they'd have to haul me to jail. (Peshkin 1986: 6)

The Christian faith may further argue that exposure to varying
perspectives would pose a serious threat to their Christian way of
life. This strong conviction does not, however, make it more
compelling to accommodate the wishes of that faith community.
In fact, it highlights the need to ensure that those children receive
an adequate education that allows them the capacity to exit that
community should they later choose to do so.

The self-acknowledged insular and totalizing practices of
Bethany Baptist Academy are illustrative of unreasonable and
intolerable conduct in a community. The vulnerability and
dependency of children require special protection to ensure that
they have the capacities to be free and equal persons. Bethany
Baptist Academy overtly constrains the child's development in
limiting their exposure to opportunities and learning objectives, it
overtly limits the child's capacity to have a capacity for the conception of the good.

Conclusion
Reasonable pluralism provides an evaluative framework to discern
permissible and impermissible community practices in relation to
school policy and practice. Numerous communities both within
schools, and external to schools, foster liberal educational aims and
are encouraged within the boundaries of reasonable pluralism.
Other community influences are in tension with liberal ideals, but
can be accommodated so long as they do not compromise liberal
educational aims. It is only when communities do not wish to
imbue *any* liberal values both in their private lives and in their
children's schooling, that they cause concern for liberal educators.
In those cases, the state is justified in setting certain regulations
that ensure that the child receives an education that facilitates their
development as free and equal persons.

The three case studies – the Anglo-European School, the
Muslim faith community and the Bethany Baptist Academy –
illustrate how liberal principles can inform school policy. Ideally
over time, liberals hope that all schools will facilitate a child's
development and exercise as an autonomous person. Given current non-ideal circumstances, some parents may wish to have their

child inducted into a particular faith and supported through faith schooling. Even in these circumstances, liberal principles can provide an evaluative mechanism to justify constraining only those community practices that inhibit a child's autonomy. This may involve some state interference in order to secure a child's autonomy. While these constraints and limitations may be unacceptable to some (such as Bethany Baptist Academy), the limitations can be justified within the principles of justice and the boundaries of reasonable pluralism in liberal theory.

Having illustrated how we can apply liberal principles to assess permissible and impermissible community practices, I now wish to promote a liberal conception of communities that develop and exercise a child's capacity for a conception of the good, and a capacity for a sense of justice.

Notes

1. For a direct link to their international participation, visit the website at: http://www.angloeuropean.essex.sch.uk/interweb/cosmos.htm
2. For a developed argument for why the French state is unjustified in banning conspicuous religious symbols, see Gereluk 2005.
3. Limiting hymns and religious songs would not apply if the Muslim students were attending a particular faith school. It seems unreasonable for a Catholic school, for example, to limit songs that are of a religious nature, when the specific mandate of the school is to promote the Catholic faith. Limiting songs of a religious nature in state education, however, seems entirely appropriate.
4. It is for this reason that 'Truth' is capitalized, as it takes on a dimension of absolute certainty.
5. 'So then faith cometh by hearing, and hearing by the word of God' is the passage that Bethany Baptist uses to justify the rationale for a compulsory speech class. (Romans 10.17)
6. The insularity is not something that the school sees as being as inflammatory or derogatory. The school wishes to insulate and protect their students from external influences. They acknowledge the narrow curricular focus, and the explicit Christian religious message – an aim that they are proud to defend.

CHAPTER 7

Liberal Communities in Schools

In the previous chapter I applied principles of reasonable pluralism to evaluate permissible and impermissible community practices in schools. However, I do not suggest that this is all that we can gain from a liberal perspective in our understanding of community. Liberal principles provide not only an evaluative mechanism, but also inform educators in how to promote communities that develop and exercise a child's capacity for a conception of the good and a capacity for a sense of justice. Although I would be remiss to suggest that this is the only conception of community that schools may promote – multiple rich and robust communities are found in schools and in schools' relation to their local communities – I contend that fostering a liberal community in schools is a minimum threshold that should be sought.

Recall that liberal principles fall within two higher order interests: a capacity for the conception of the good, and a capacity for a sense of justice. A capacity for a conception of the good entails having the capacity 'to have, to revise, and rationally to pursue a conception of the good' (Rawls 2001: 19). A capacity for a sense of justice is the 'capacity to understand, to apply, and to act from (and not merely in accordance with) the principles of political justice that specify the fair terms of social cooperation' (ibid.: 18–19). I develop a liberal conception of community that enhances these aims, and the corresponding benefits of doing so for children. The first section of the chapter will be devoted to the direct ways in which a child benefits from her exposure to and participation in a liberal community.

The second section of the chapter considers the role schools may have in promoting a capacity for a sense of justice in society. As I argued in Chapter 5, the basic structure of society, through the underpinning principles within the fair terms of social co-operation, realizes a distinctive community with implicit moral values. I justify why schools should promote communities that promote dispositions within the fair terms of social cooperation to foster children's capacity for a sense of justice in a liberal society.

A capacity for a conception of the good

This section examines particular community practices that promote a child's capacity for a conception of the good. Specifically, I consider communities that expose children to various opportunities and experiences, communities that develop children's capacity to belong, participate and negotiate their way in a group, and realize communities that provide value in children in developing certain affiliations and loyalties to other people and associations as part of their capacity for a conception of the good. The first aspect addresses the need for children to have sufficient opportunities to participate in communities that will expose them to potentially valuable experiences afforded to them through various communal associations. The second aspect recognizes that 'persons' conception of the good are not fixed but form and develop as they mature, and may change more or less radically over the course of life' (Rawls 1993: 20). The third addresses the flourishing that individuals may have in their devotions and attachments to other people in our relation to our world (ibid.: 16). Communities that promote these liberal ideals are integral to a child's development as autonomous individuals.

Schools facilitate a child's development and exercise for a capacity for a conception of the good in numerous ways: most obviously, through skills and knowledge taught in the formal curriculum. Yet also, prevalent community activities in schools provide a vital role in a child's capacity for a conception of the good. One purpose of promoting communities in schools is to broaden a child's exposure to various perspectives and ways of life. When children enter school, they bring with them the perspectives that have been shared within their local communal circle, most commonly comprising family and those within their parents' communities. Schools, however, provide a bridge between the child's limited exposure within the family, to broader and multiple communities in society. We hope that schools are seen as a link to the broader community, bringing the experiences of the wider society to that of the child.

It is likely that many children will naturally broaden their participation in communities as they mature. Given this, it might be argued that schools do not need to provide communal activities that expose children to various perspectives if children can learn this in their day-to-day experiences. However, we must also account for children who may have limited access to varied communities, either through communities that discourage alternative ways of thinking, or due to socio-economic factors that inhibit their access to various communities. Given these social circumstances, schools become a convenient place to facilitate the promotion of community. It is in these cases that we find a compelling reason for schools to ensure that all children have the opportunity to belong to a range of communities.

Consider, for example, a child that is brought up in a community that purposely tries to inhibit alternative ways of thinking and living. The Christian fundamentalist community is one such example in which the members' intention is to shelter their children's exposure to other ways of living. A child who is not exposed to alternative perspectives is limited in her capacity to pursue or revise a conception of the good. While the state does not overtly ban the Christian fundamentalists' community, the state does have a responsibility to ensure that those children have the capacity to make informed decisions about how they wish to lead their lives as free and equal persons. Schools can be an effective way to ensure that children learn about alternative perspectives.

Similarly, it is not uncommon for economically disadvantaged students to have a limited exposure to a variety of experiences and ways of living. There may be a variety of social and economic factors that contribute to this impoverished, closed community life. Economically disadvantaged families may not have the resources to enrol their children in various clubs and community groups that broaden a child's experience. For example, they may not have the finances to enrol their children in music, sports or various youth groups. Families may further not have the resources or time to take their children to various events such as museums, social or cultural events and concerts – all of which may broaden a child's perspective of the world, which is larger than their immediate community surroundings.

Other families may have lower levels of social capital. They may be unable to negotiate or engage in particular activities that would broaden their children's experience, either because of their lower competencies in language comprehension, education levels or socio-economic status. These disadvantages may intimidate parents from participating in their outer surroundings, and they may feel safer in closer, confined settings (or within their homogeneous grouping). These are but a few possible reasons why children may be limited in their choices to belong to and participate in communities.

Other families may not have the time available to devote to their children in ways that would expand their ways of knowing and understanding the diversity of human experience. Parents may work long hours, in shift work or at too irregular times to be able to foster enriching experiences for their children. Further, even when parents do have spare time, they may not necessarily see the value in exposing their children to alternative perspectives. Simply, when given the chance to enrol their child in a community group, they may not have the motivation, will or energy.

In these instances, we see that schools can provide children with opportunities to be exposed to and participate in different communities. It is important to emphasize both aspects of exposure and participation: simply exposing children to varied ways of living may not be enough to secure a capacity for a conception of the good. The prime reason is that children who may be exposed to alternative ways of living may have a conception of other ways of living, but it may not be in their power to revise their present circumstances. Brighouse notes that 'equipping people with the skills needed rationally to reflect on alternative choices about how to live is a crucial component of providing them with substantive freedom and opportunities, by enabling them to make better rather than worse choices about how to live their lives' (2000a: 80). Participation in a community can be a key element in fostering each child's capacity to pursue and revise the kind of life she wishes to lead as an autonomous individual.

Bethany Baptist Academy illustrates this point. If we consider hypothetically a change in the school policy whereby teachers are required to teach alternative perspectives, this in and of itself alone may not be sufficient for children to choose an alternative lifestyle different from Christian fundamentalism. Although teachers would expose children to different perspectives, they might not necessarily encourage them to consider pursuing those perspectives as a viable option. It is conceivable that children who wish to pursue different aims that are in conflict with those of the school would be met with trepidation, disapproval or hostility. If the school is to be sincere about allowing an openness to explore and experience other ways of living, exposure to various communities may not be sufficient.[1]

Participation in a community, rather than mere exposure, is a position that MacIntyre (1981) holds as being vital to understanding the complexities and richness within that community. He argues that in order to understand the richness of traditions of a particular community one cannot simply observe it from the outside, but must be inducted into the internal practices of that community. To observe the traditions of a community from an external perspective would not bring out the richness of the internal practices within the community. For instance, teaching about religion from a curricular text in order for children to have the capacity to view alternative ways of living would not be effective from MacIntyre's perspective. Curricular emphases that teach children about different cultures and traditions may broaden their awareness of various communal lives, but they would not necessarily bring out the depth and richness of the culture. To understand the traditions, customs and practices of a community, one needs to be an active member of that community.

To illustrate this point, one can use the analogy of looking at a stained glass church window from the outside and again from the inside. An individual who looks at the stained glass window from the outside sees the various colours and patterns, but, from afar, they may be nondescript or, in a word, unspectacular.[2] However, once the individual enters the church and looks at the same church window with the sun shining through the pane, the individual is able to see the brilliance of the window, with the stained pattern illuminating across the church floor, reflecting the light in its various radiance. The windowpane becomes spectacular and awe-inspiring, only to be marvelled at by those who are on the inside. The outside observer sees the pattern, but will never be able to see its potential grand brilliance. MacIntyre views community in a similar manner. To view a particular tradition from the outside, a person can see the dominant traits and characteristics, but not completely understand the nuances and charms that internal members value. While it is (conceivably) very difficult to induct children into various community practices in school to provide the internal scope and depth of which MacIntyre speaks, his argument lends itself toward purposeful, meaningful community experiences that enrich a child's life.

Similarly, the development of habits through experience in education is a main concept in Dewey's (1916) thinking.

Experience should be thought of as 'purposeful doing' that enlarges children's perceptions of themselves and the world, enriching themselves through experience, and eventually formulating and negotiating these experiences to maximize their potential (ibid.: 185): conversely, ordinary experience that does not elevate, inspire or is put forth in a mediocre fashion would 'weaken vigor and efficiency of thought' (ibid.: 61). For Dewey, learning community is not a passive engagement. Communities are not an abstract concept taught from textbooks on how 'other' people live; this would not be meaningful for the child, nor would it be an effective pedagogical strategy. Children learn community by participating in community.

The principles behind Dewey's vision parallel liberal thought. Active student participation through community is aimed at providing the meaningful connections and associations needed to function in society. Active participation in communal activities expands on the child's upbringing in the home, and broadens it to wider communal contexts found in school and society. The multiple experiences and connections that are made available in schools play a pivotal role in the facilitation of children's autonomy.

Both MacIntyre and Dewey illustrate the role that schools play in providing meaningful opportunities for students to participate in and understand communities from within. The manifestation of communities that broaden a child's experience beyond the parameters of their local familial structure need not be overwhelming. In many cases, schools already provide opportunities for children to be exposed to communal dispositions in their daily experience of schools.

The early formative years of schooling devote a large proportion of time to cultivating social development and the child's awareness of others. Early childhood education often emphasizes certain cooperative dispositions in the classroom. It teaches about the role of sharing, taking turns in class, discussing problems and working things out among themselves, and making children aware of the consequences of one's actions on others. Further, we simulate activities that help children to learn these cooperative skills. During playtime, we may have a toy house set up where children can role-play. There may be puppet theatres and costume areas where children can learn to play together and imagine situations where they may have to work out a problem and arrive at a solution. Further, story time and sharing circles help cultivate speaking and listening skills, and being attentive to one another in a respectful and orderly manner. These skills and activities help to form the basis for learning how to be cooperative.

While the pedagogic role at this stage does not yet create formal communities, it sets the foundations for teaching children how to interact with others and create the beginnings of community. Young children have a limited sense of the world beyond their immediate circles. Through exposure to positive forms of social development over a period of time, it is possible to broaden the child's perspectives to see how they should live in a world that encompasses both the interests of themselves and others. These early school years provide the foundations for developing dispositions conducive to reciprocity and mutuality essential to the fair terms of social cooperation in a well-ordered society.

Once these foundations begin to form, schools may create various types of communal activities in which students can participate in extra-curricular activities. The younger years in primary school are often devoted to cooperative or more passive activities that are easier to negotiate. Children may be involved in choral clubs, drama activities and art clubs that encourage a particular interest in a collaborative manner.

Often athletic clubs are introduced in the middle years of primary schools and at the secondary level where higher-level skills may be required to balance the role of participation and sportsmanship with the competitive nature of such games. Although a primary aim of a child may be to develop a certain skill in a particular activity, it also requires learning rules and regulations that are implicit through one's participation in community. Further, the participation in a particular group provides opportunities for that child to experience and explore interests and develop their skills.

We see the particular benefits of children's participation in music, athletics or language, where there may be a particular advantage in learning these skills at a younger age, rather than later in life. The provision of these activities in schools ensures that all children have access to these activities, which can provide access into these communities. For example, a child who learns a foreign language has greater access to other cultures. She is able to communicate in another language, opening connections and opportunities. She has a better chance of understanding the different perspectives of people who speak that language.

Extracurricular clubs such as environmental groups, peace

groups and groups that support a particular charity or particular aid, expose children to broader complex issues of social justice in the public sphere. Schools may develop an international link with another school from another region or country and develop bonds between the two schools. These sorts of groups and projects help children to see how their participation and activism may influence or change attitudes within and beyond their school. Aid to a particular charity shows how students' contributions and efforts have direct positive results for those who receive their assistance. Children may come to understand the complexity of issues and ways of influence by participating in environmental and peace movements. By creating and modelling communities that are present in adult society, such community activism may help to provide a transition for children who are interested in specific goals and who may wish to continue them in their adult years.

In all of these activities one becomes inducted into a particular community with others that share similar interests and values. Participation in some activities is more explicit in their communal focus, such as team sports, or extracurricular clubs that bring individuals together for a common purpose. However, these opportunities allow children to engage with other individuals who share common interests. The communal bonds that are formed in the process distinguish it from other general aims of schooling. Schools have a specific role in providing communities for children to enter and in which they can participate, in order that they can a) experience different ways of thinking and living, and b) find other individuals who share common interests and values. Put together, children's participation in communities helps to facilitate their capacity for a conception of the good.

Given the numerous ways in which schools may provide opportunities for children to participate in communities, one might ask what is the minimum threshold that schools must provide in order to facilitate a child's capacity for a conception of the good? I am well aware that it is near impossible to expose children to every alternative way of life and expose them to every type of community. For instance, children who live in rural communities may have less heterogeneous communities within their local demographics, or may have fewer resources to devote to provide various communities. This is an important considera-tion. However, what we may instead advocate is a threshold level of alternative ways of participating and belonging to alternative ways of living. If persons live in a more autonomy facilitating society, schools might not need to play such a large role. Conversely, those children who live in a more closed society may require the external influence of schools to provide alternative ways of life. This would be a more practical and realistic conception to implement.

Again, there may be disagreements about what that threshold level might entail. In principle, schools that promote various clubs and activities help to broaden a child's parameters of thinking of how she may wish to lead a life that is to her benefit. If we believe this principle, then it follows that children will be disadvantaged if schools do not have extracurricular activities, which allow children to explore various types of school communities. And where schools might not have the facilities or resources, we might recommend that children have access to particular types of experiences either at another nearby school, or at a local participating community club. It is therefore not necessary to have every school provide athletics, performing arts, languages and other community clubs, but we must attempt to have a range of communal activities that are accessible for children to participate in should they so wish.

The provision of communities in schools is one that cannot be underestimated in developing children's capacity for a conception of the good. Children need to have opportunities to participate in communities where they have a sense of belonging or comfort with others. As I explained in Chapter 4, such communities bring value to people's lives through their shared common interests, and provide identity and moral orientation for individuals. We further learn accepted norms and behaviours through our participation in established communal relations. These social relations are often key factors in a person's conception of the good. If we assume that individuals value social connectedness to others, then it is reasonable to suggest that schools provide opportunities to foster and enhance such communal opportunities for children. Schools are a potentially effective way in which to provide varied communities that will allow children to pursue different options.

A capacity for a sense of justice and a well-ordered society

The promotion of communities in schools serves a second, and equally important function from a liberal perspective. Not only are liberals concerned about having sufficient opportunities for children to participate in communities in exposing them to a range of beliefs and interests, they also are interested in developing particular dispositions that: ensure a capacity for a sense of justice; and develop dispositions of reciprocity that underpin the basic structure of society within the fair terms of social cooperation. There may be other important benefits that children learn from their participation in communities, as I have outlined in Chapter 4. While the benefits derived from community may far out-number the dispositions that I list here (and goods that liberals may find valuable), the dispositions that liberals are particularly concerned about are those that underpin a well-ordered society. In Rawls' final work, he acknowledges that:

> a political society is a community if we now mean by a community a society, including a political society, the members of which – in this case citizens – share certain final ends to which they give very high priority, so much so that in stating before themselves the kind of person they want to be they count their having these ends as essential ... *What is vital is that the well-ordered society specified by the political con-ception of justice characterizes citizens as having shared final ends of the requisite kind.* [emphasis added] (Rawls 2001: 199–200)

The second aim of promoting liberal communities in schools is to develop and exercise a child's capacity for a sense of justice within the overarching political community.

A number of factors arise in securing individuals' capacity for a sense of justice. First, individuals need to be informed about rules and regulations that will have direct impact on their lives. Second, individuals should have substantive opportunities to participate in public matters if they so choose. Third, a critical threshold of citizens must participate in the public sphere of a society in order that the political community does not disintegrate. Finally, should individuals wish to re-enter public deliberation, there should be protective mechanisms in place to enable them to do so. Whereas the communities fostered in the previous section address myriad communities underneath a liberal society, these factors address the overarching political community.

The first factor involves teaching students the overarching political structure of society. This is the civic component within a liberal conception of community. Students should be taught the rules and regulations in which public policy is developed. A formal curricular objective can address this aspect by teaching the basic structures found in society – those of political, social and financial institutions – and the processes by which each work. The citizenship curriculum addresses this aspect in the National Curriculum, which focuses on the governmental processes found in liberal societies.

Another effective way to teach students about the rules and regulations within society is to have active student governance in schools that parallel political procedures found in liberal society. Student councils commonly have an adult supervisor who provides guidance as to the procedural mechanisms found in political institutions. Student councils often raise student concerns that arise in the school, and help provide support and activities for the student body to enjoy. The processes of the student council are usually modelled after government procedures, and in this way provide students with an introduction to the democratic processes and procedures that are in place within local and national political institutions.

A stronger conception of student participation is to integrate student governance within the structure of the larger governing board of the school. Weaker conceptions often leave student councils on the periphery of school governance, focusing mainly on student concerns and student activities. Integrating student governance into the school policy structures, however, is more inclusive. Some schools have direct student representation within the governing structure of the school. Other forms of student participation in the governance of the school may include student body votes that determine school policies. Heads of school may consult with student representatives for their perspective on school issues. Some heads may have regular forms of question/answer forums in which to raise various school issues that affect the student body. Being committed to student participation helps to give students an effective 'voice' and 'vote' in policy matters. If children can see how their involvement may influence others in a meaningful forum, then it may help show children how their participation in greater public affairs can be effective through local and civic activism.

The second factor addresses teaching students various mechanisms in which to participate in public matters. Communities can be an instrumental and effective means to influence and lobby public issues in society. Young (2000) argues that deliberative democracy may help to reduce the structural injustices that formal political equality cannot alleviate on its own. Broadening political inclusion through associational participation may foster greater social justice in society. When combined with norms of political equality, 'inclusion allows for maximum expression of interests, opinions, and perspectives relevant to the problems or issues for which a public seeks solutions' (ibid.: 23).

Young does acknowledge that communities have multiple hierarchies, with different interests and ideological commitments. She further contends that using community toward an idea of a 'common good' may serve as a means of exclusion, highlighting only dominant norms of those groups. Despite this problem, she suggests that minorities and under-represented groups may still prefer to form a collective group in which to have more influence in the public sphere than if they were not to have any collective action. Freedom of association and a civic culture that allows for individuals to deliberate about public issues is at least one way to have input into decisions that will affect people's lives. Community may prove to be a best mechanism in a non-ideal situation.

Given that many communities play a fundamental role in deliberating in public matters, children should be aware of the potential of public participation through communities. A pedagogic role of schools would be to teach students various means to influence and contribute to the political structure of society: involvement in communities is one effective way in which to participate. In many cases, community groups and collective action are at the forefront in raising the profile of public issues and exerting political pressure at the institutional level.

The Anglo-European School has taken an active stance in providing opportunities for students to see how their involvement in communities can influence public policy. The school's participation in various organizations such as Amnesty International, AIDS Awareness, Landmine Action, the United Nations Association, WorldWatch and UNICEF provide opportunities for students to see how collective action can make a substantive difference in public affairs. While liberals would be hesitant to insist upon students' mandatory participation in communities, students should have substantive opportunities to become involved if they so choose.

The third factor – that of ensuring a critical threshold of citizens' participation in the political structure of society – is more difficult to address directly at the school level. This is a larger societal question of how to encourage individuals to participate in the public political matters in society. With decreasing voter participation and an increasing perception of apathy toward the political structure, this problem has been relegated to schools to try to increase civic activism among youth.

Taylor (1995b) suggests that the liberal political system requires rebalancing by increasing civic participation. He argues that communities contribute to greater democratic processes in that:

(a) the people concerned understand themselves as belonging to a community that shares some common purposes and recognizes its members as sharing in these purposes;

(b) the various groups, types and classes of citizens have been given a genuine hearing and were able to have an impact on the debate; and

(c) the decision emerging from this is really the majority preference. (ibid.: 276)

He suggests that in societies where individuals are compelled only by their individual self-interests, only (b) and (c) may emerge, and even then, he suggests that (c) alone may be the possible result. Taylor challenges the fair terms of social cooperation in its ideal theory in questioning how the rules and regulations upon which all individuals will mutually agree can be decided when only thin common aims are apparent. The requirement of (a) helps identify what is meaningful for individuals in a particular society. In order to decide what is best for developing such normative principles as the basis for social justice in society, we begin to tread not only on the preferred outcomes, but the processes through which we come to those decisions.

Yet, mandating public participation, a position Taylor advocates, is problematic for a number of reasons. The first difficulty fails to recognize that real opportunity costs are involved in an individual's participation in community and other public affairs. Public participation takes time and energy, which has real costs to an individual in terms of less time spent with their family, work or other leisure activities. Enforcing greater public participation in collective matters infringes individuals' opportunity to make choices to opt out of the public sphere within their conception of the good. Some people, simply, may not wish to join communities or become involved in the public affairs of society. If individuals choose to opt out of the public deliberations (assuming that they are informed rational adults), they do so trusting that others will act on their behalf in good faith. If we are to respect individuals as free and equal, then we also need to respect their choice not to participate.

That being said, while it might be argued that adults should not be enforced to mandate public participation, it may be reasonable for children to learn how to participate in community as part of their development towards a capacity for a sense of justice. Children need to learn about the choices afforded to them as public citizens, but they also require to be exposed to such options. Conceivably, schools may address this in at least two ways. One approach might teach that participating in public matters contributes to a robust liberal society, and similarly, a lack of participation may threaten the basis upon which the political structure is based. Case studies of voter trends and their corresponding implications for a political institution may illustrate the relevance of participation in public affairs. Similarly, teaching students about various public movements such as the suffragettes, civic movements, labour movements and apartheid are demonstrative of the political influence and the effectiveness of collective action within the political arena.

The second possibility is to make community service a compulsory component within education. While we might argue that mandating community service for adults would impose on their autonomy as free and equal persons, we might believe that students' participation would facilitate their capacity to participate in public activism should they so choose as adults.

I want to be cautious in supporting the latter proposal as a way in which to build a critical threshold of public participation in society. In principle, community service may be an effective way to provide students with meaningful experiences of public participation. However, the present implementation of community service components does have some notably contentious points.

The first concerns the idea that schools should alleviate the perceived ills of society. The difficulty of decreased voter turnout and a perceived increase of political apathy is one that liberal societies have acknowledged, yet have found difficult to resolve. The Australian compulsory voting procedures, for instance, have not necessarily helped to foster greater political activism within its citizenry. Some individuals purposely spoil their ballot in protest; others choose candidates who are offering a 'joke' agenda. Concern about an increasingly apathetic citizenry, in many states, has brought renewed emphasis toward placing the responsibility back onto schools to address this problem. But why should schools be responsible for this burden? States have demonstrated little success in revitalizing political activism, yet have little difficulty shifting this responsibility to schools. This shift of responsibilities should not be taken for granted. An increase in public participation may require something much broader than what schools alone can realistically provide.

The second concerns the implementation of current community service initiatives. One of the common criticisms expressed by students who are involved in a citizenship project is that, while the programme tries to encourage youth involvement in the local community, the local community does not have a reciprocal trust in youth. Mistrust by police and other public services is perceived by young people who, in turn, feel that they cannot trust them to assist them when they are in need of help (Gardner, Lawton and Cairns 2000). Similarly, many local stores have discriminatory policies whereby students are not allowed to enter the store without an adult, and regularly youths are denied access onto buses. Schools may attempt to embrace and develop closer ties to their community, but if the external environment does not reciprocate and reflect these similar aims then it will be difficult to achieve meaningful associations between students and their local environment. Again, increasing public participation in youth will meet limited success if society is not sincere in forming a reciprocal level of trust.

A community service component may fulfil the following: to develop students' capacities to develop a capacity for a sense of justice through public participation; to create a community service component that is collaborative and reciprocal with the local community; and to develop a meaningful experience for the student. Sensitivity to these liberal principles would be required before we could endorse a compulsory community service element.

Finally, the fourth factor of securing a capacity for a sense of justice involves securing protective mechanisms should individuals wish to re-enter public deliberation at any given point. This is not a protection that schools can provide, other than through developing capacities in children that facilitate their ability to enter public deliberation should they so choose as adults.

In addressing the first three factors, schools can address an important component of facilitating children's capacity for a sense of justice. The second component within a liberal community, although not completely separate from the first set of factors, is teaching dispositions of reciprocity within the fair terms of social cooperation. As I argued earlier, the fair terms of social co-operation have implicit moral values that create a distinctive political community. Reciprocity is an interpersonal disposition that calls for individuals being fair to someone, in the expressed hope that they will be fair to them (Rawls 2001: 196). This is a key disposition that underpins the aspect of social cooperation.

Reciprocity is a key aspect for building trust and confidence between persons. People who understand and adhere to the notion of reciprocity will develop increased levels of trust and confidence. It is a natural feature of reciprocity to become more trustful in those who have agreed upon similar terms of engagement and respect that you in turn would give to them. Reciprocity plays an important role in the stability of a just society as the agreed upon rules and regulations that are the basis for a well-ordered society rest upon this disposition. Rawls sums up it up as follows:

> The trust and confidence ... grow stronger and more complete as the success of shared cooperative arrangements is sustained over a longer time; and they also grow stronger and more complete when the basic institutions framed to secure fundamental interests (for example, the basic rights and liberties) are more willingly and steadfastly recognized in public political life. (Rawls 2001: 196)

The shared cooperative arrangements, to which Rawls refers, I suggest, are a particular liberal conception of community.

If the political arrangement of a well-ordered society rests upon the fair terms of social cooperation, an essential aim in the development of a child is to learn and develop dispositions of reciprocity. Reciprocity, as I argued in Chapter 5, cannot be learnt in isolation. Children must have substantive opportunities to participate in communities to see how the aspect of reciprocity is both beneficial and important.

One might contend that reciprocity does not necessarily need to be learnt through community, but could be learnt by alternative means. Simple daily interactions might suffice, or reading parables and stories that exemplify the disposition may be sufficient. While these means may have some effect, I contend that reciprocity entails something more than mere informal interactions with other people. To understand the weight of reciprocity involves having some sustained relations with other people with some vested interest toward similar purposes or goals. The process of having to work through difficult scenarios in practice and come to some agreed upon aims, exhibits the importance of reciprocity.

This is a difficult concept to teach to young children who may not understand the need to follow particular rules and regulations within a group within a notion of reciprocity. Yet, modelling this behaviour through participation in a community is an essential aspect to developing this disposition. Unlike informal interactions whereby reciprocity is possible but limited, the long-term benefits of reciprocity may be more apparent through sustained relationships that are found in communities. Similarly, children will also be able to see the repercussions of breaking reciprocity: diminished trust and confidence among the members will result, with similar negative effects on the stability of a community.

Again, children's participation in communities outside school can also expose them to the disposition of reciprocity. However, schools are in the advantageous position explicitly to highlight the disposition of reciprocity while children are participating in community. An effective pedagogical practice might, for instance, reflect upon the ethos of a community, pointing out how established and sustained reciprocity will provide a healthy and stable community. Similarly, when reciprocity is broken, teachers can show the subsequent consequences to the children. This conscious reflection is a key component in developing children's dispositions of reciprocity.

Teaching reciprocity through children's participation in community does not necessarily require forming new communities in schools; rather, it is an explicit disposition that should be prevalent in the communities that are already offered in schools. For instance, if a school offers sports clubs in which children can participate, the aspect of reciprocity can be developed through the shared interest of sports. Reciprocity is a key component in all healthy communities, and should be highlighted as such by schools. Therefore, schools do not yet have to develop communities for the expressed purpose of developing reciprocity, but should make it explicit in the communities that they already offer.

One exception to this, however, is in developing children's dispositions of reciprocity through participation in specific local communities. Formal curricular instruction for older youth would be important in making the connection of reciprocity at the local level to the essential function of reciprocity within the larger political structure. Comparing ideal political structures in society with those of non-ideal political structures in relatively stable and unstable countries would illustrate the fundamental role of reciprocity in a well-ordered society.

Conclusion

Schools that foster liberal communities address two main points: communities that facilitate a child's development and exercise for a capacity for a conception of the good and a capacity for a sense of justice. This is a minimum threshold of provision that is necessary if we are to secure these two higher order principles. Other communities may provide goods. So long as those communities are not in conflict with liberal principles, they too would be allowable within a liberal conception of community. However, the essential component of promoting community within a liberal conception is that they facilitate children's development as free and equal persons. Schools facilitate opportunities for children to participate in various communities that will help to develop and exercise their capacity for a conception of the good in three ways: communities provide opportunities for children to be exposed to alternative shared interests and values; children's participation in varied communal experiences helps to secure their ability to pursue and reject which communities they wish to be a part of during the course of their life; and communities provide intrinsic goods to persons.

Secondly, liberals are concerned with children's development of a capacity for a sense of justice. Teaching about the overarching political community is a necessary component in children's development as autonomous individuals. Underlying this is the fundamental disposition of reciprocity within the fair terms of social cooperation.

The theoretical framework that I have developed from Rawls' liberal theory provides an evaluative component for communities that are permissible in schools within a plural society, and offers guidance for policy and practice for the minimum required provision of particular communities in schools.

In Part III, I return to the non-ideal circumstances of promoting community in schools given external societal pressures and internal educational practices. I explore these challenges, and consider alternative possibilities that may create conducive conditions for liberal communities.

Notes

1. Of course, the types of communities that schools could condone would be limited within the limits of reasonable pluralism. We would not, for instance, wish schools to foster groups that encourage prejudice, such as in the case of gangs.
2. Many thanks to Terry McLaughlin from whom I first heard of this analogy.

PART III

Community, Schools and Society

CHAPTER 8

Communities and Society

Current social conditions in civil society influence the formation of communities. Communities have never been fixed or ossified, but are constantly changing and evolving. Even traditional and homogeneous communities are negotiated by their members, and are influenced by external factors. To understand the evolving nature of communities from agrarian to contemporary society, I examine the work of Ferdinand Tönnies who observed the changing facets of communities during the Industrial Revolution. His depiction of the changing social condition can be seen as a pivotal work among sociologists who grapple with the notion of community. I begin with his analysis as a backdrop to the contemporary social order and its effects on communities, after which I turn to contemporary social theorists to examine contemporary civil society and its implications for communities.

As I mentioned in Chapter 4, Putnam's book, *Bowling Alone*, suggests that there has been a steady decline of communities in American civil society. His thesis is partly correct. Traditional forms of communities and associations that were prominent in the beginning to the mid-twentieth century have weakened. However, new communities are emerging. I explore these trends and note the challenges and opportunities that arise during this transitional period.

Tensions due to a diminished individual interest in civil society are palpable and disconcerting at times. Yet, these uncertain periods also mark the potential for new possibilities and opportunities. I conclude by touching upon how some of these civil upheavals can make way for communities that promote liberal principles.

From feudal to modern society: the changing dynamics of community

The Industrial Revolution markedly changed the social structure of society. People, who previously may have worked in cottage industries and in agriculture, were now moving away from the homestead to urban centres. New elements of modernization irrevocably changed the workplace. Cottage industries gave way to larger, more efficient factories. The introduction of the assembly line meant that products could be made cheaper and faster than could be achieved under previous techniques.

These changes in the workplace had considerable ripple effects in all other aspects of civil society. Observing these great changes taking place, Tönnies (1957) examined the effects of the Industrial Revolution on communities. He was troubled by what he saw as the dissipation of *Gemeinschaft*: communities based on kinship, neighbourliness and friendship. In its place was the proliferation of *Gesellschaft*: a more transitory and superficial aspect of community based on rational will and economic advantage.

Gemeinschaft was a pre-social condition, and one that was to be valued as essential to civil society. People did not come to agreement or consensus; rather, mutual understanding was the starting point of togetherness. The strongest of such bonds could be seen in three types of relationships, namely: '(1) the relation between a mother and her child; (2) relation between husband and wife in its natural or general biological state; (3) the relation among brothers and sisters, that is, at least among those who know each other as being the offspring of the same mother' (ibid.: 42). These would provide the multiple sources of understanding, and from this foundation they would provide the stability and health of a society. This *Gemeinschaft* kind of understanding preceded all agreements and disagreements, and was the starting point of all togetherness.

Gesellschaft, on the other hand, is not brought together by kinship and neighbourliness, but out of a necessity to associate with others who may be of advantage to them. It is an artificially constructed association, and one that is developed for a specific reason. The association is not one of kinship and friendship, but of agonistic necessity. The relationships formed serve a purpose, but do not necessarily start from a point of mutual understanding. The individual enters a relationship of free choice (as opposed to the *Gemeinschaft* relationship) in order to derive some value in being part of that relationship.

With the advance of industrialization, Tönnies saw the upheaval of *Gemeinschaft* communities, during which individuals would move away from their families. This detrimental turn would have significant and negative implications for civil society. How could people have a collective will and common good, when the proliferation of *Gesellschaft*-like associations was becoming more commonplace? While roads were being built to connect individuals from one town to another, the relationships and connections within the enlarged towns themselves were decaying.[1]

Tönnies' analysis was a heavy and pessimistic forewarning for modern society. The changes in civil society with industrialization had tremendous implications for traditional feudal communities. Although Tönnies wrote in the age of the Industrial Revolution, elements of his thesis still resonate in the examination of changing communities. Communities were vastly changing with the advance of industrialization, and new forms of associations were being developed.

Yet, to portray only the weakening of *Gemeinschaft* communities during the nineteenth century would not be entirely accurate. Other movements began to form in their place, ones that addressed the changing social conditions marked by the Industrial Age. Having said this, history has shown that there are particular points in history that resisted and challenged the dominant trends of the Industrial Revolution in hopes of retaining and building strong communities.

Communities have not become defunct since the advent of the Industrial Revolution, but have modified according to the social needs and changing demands of civil society. The dissipation of the *Gemeinschaft* community in feudal society was one that Tönnies feared. Yet, the twentieth century saw the creation of new communities, often more diverse and widespread than would be possible in feudal conditions.

The nature of communities in modern society has been one of marked change and evolution. The next section examines the proliferation of non-profit community organizations during the beginning to the mid-twentieth century, and their general downturn of membership over the last thirty years.

Social conditions and communities in contemporary society

The concern about the loss of communities in society has been debated of late. Putnam's (2000) book, *Bowling Alone*, has sparked the debate and concern about the dwindling memberships of communities in American society. Drawing upon social and political trends in the United States, Putnam argues that Americans have become increasingly disconnected from their families, friends, neighbourhoods and other social structures that provide networks and connections between people.

One effect of people's increased economic pursuits, such as increased work hours, is that other leisure activities will accordingly fall (Hirsch 1977). An accumulation of individual demands and wants has placed greater emphasis on better economic growth. This may translate into increased work hours per day, or greater pursuit of promotion at work. The option of either increasing the amount of resources through work, or by working with one's already available goods, however, results in diminished time elsewhere. Individuals' attempts to increase their positional advantage will have real opportunity costs in terms of leisure activities, such as participating in communities, meeting up with friends and families, and other social activities. One cannot change the number of hours in a day, and one's priorities will reflect their preferences. The pressure to do more things with the same amount of time has led, however, to some unintended effects.

One of the direct costs is that the aspect of friendship and communal relations is adversely affected. Developing and maintaining networks among people takes time:

> The impact of time pressures on sociability – in the sense of friendliness, social contact, and mutual concern – is made particularly severe by the fact that these social relationships do not, by their nature, have the character of private economic goods: which is to say that the costs and benefits of specific actions do not fall primarily on those undertaking them. (Hirsch 1977: 78)

Social interactions have come under increasing strain due to increased desires toward individual 'time-absorbing consumption' and 'positional competition' (ibid.: 81). In a consumer-oriented society, being sociable in communal activities is becoming more difficult.

The trend that suggests people are entering into fewer communal relations is cause for concern for individuals and for civil society. The concern is that individuals who have fewer networks and connections tend to have less social capital. Social capital, Putnam contends, is a strong indicator of quality of life for individuals and, consequently, for society. People with less social capital may have increased incidence of crime and poverty, lower educational attainment, higher risks of teenage pregnancy or suicide, and higher mortality. As a consequence of lower individual social capital, the stability and prosperity of society also becomes affected. Fewer communal activities and meaningful opportunities for building trust among people have detrimental effects on society.

A number of empirical studies have tried to show the effects of greater and lesser levels of social capital in society. For instance, Wilkinson (1996) contends that societies that have generally greater levels of social capital will have healthier individuals. His thesis suggests that links can be made between an individual's social interactions and health. Despite variations among healthy egalitarian societies, one common factor among all of them is social cohesion (ibid.: 4). Increased levels of welfare are created implicitly through social cohesion with others in their community. People who have greater social capital offer assistance to those in need, and ensure that they are provided for. Conversely, the greater the stress in a family and in other social support networks, the greater likelihood that one's health will suffer (ibid.: 164). For instance, one particular study suggested a correlation between unemployment and that of increased marital arguments, diminished circle of friends and a curtailment in their social life (ibid.: 164). Wilkinson concludes that the quality of social life is a powerful determinant of health (ibid.: 5).

While membership in communities and associations has declined, three countertrends have emerged suggesting a renewal of personal relationships: small informal encounter groups, various social movements and 'virtual' communities. Each of these groups addresses aspects of 'self-improvement', 'self-expression', and 'consciousness-raising' (Putnam 2000: 149). For example, while church groups have declined, small self-help groups and book clubs are gaining in support and membership. Self-help topics have gained popularity in bookstores and, similarly, there has been an increase in the number of small therapy or spiritual groups aiming to reconnect one to oneself and, in the process, connect oneself to others. These range in scope from twelve-step programmes for gamblers and alcoholics, to weight management and therapy groups. The common feature among these self-help groups is the potential to provide emotional support and inter-personal ties between participants (ibid.: 150).

Book clubs are also rising in popularity, although they have always been around since the second half of the nineteenth century. Traditionally, book clubs were created by middle-class Americans, but this has extended to other segments of the population. Although the impetus for the groups usually began as forms of intellectual 'self-improvement', some book groups evolve into areas of what Putnam refers as 'consciousness-raising' (ibid.: 149). Personal and intellectual pursuits often merge into political and social movements. The informal reading gatherings sometimes become the seeds that form grassroots social and political movements. Building people's social networks, such as reading circles, also encourages people to become involved in larger community affairs.

Finally, new communities are being formed around the Internet. 'Virtual' communities are a new phenomenon with the advent of the computer and Internet capabilities. While elements of virtual communities may arguably have existed prior to the computer (through correspondence of pen pals and organizations that held together through letters and telephone conversations), the Internet has revolutionized the notion of virtual communities. The Internet has brought people together in innumerable ways. People can join community chat groups that serve a particular interest for those members. Included among the various community sites on the Internet, one can now enter a 'community' site and find over five hundred sites to pray virtually online using the Yahoo search engine, find grief counselling and cyber romance, enter thousands of chat groups or become involved in 'virtual' protests through online petitions and action points (ibid.: 170). Numerous other community groups and networks emerge daily on the Internet and continue to connect people without leaving the confines of their computer desk.

Creating social capital through online connection, however, is a controversial consideration. Do Internet connections create greater social connectedness among people, or do they substitute for 'real' communities? Does the Internet exacerbate the social fragmentation in society by disengaging citizens from one another through an artificial construct? Further, does the non-personal communication increase the likelihood of abuse when compared with those communities formed through personal contact? In some respects, the Internet provides potential for people to become more civically connected and engaged as a result of the immediate access to information and the potential to connect to others. On the other hand, the Internet may encourage people to become more reclusive in these 'artificial' meeting spots, never to meet anyone, with the potential to further create a civic sedateness. Putnam suggests that neither scenario is probably the case: the Internet is probably not the fated 'gloom and doom' cause of civic fragmentation, nor is it the hoped-for 'brave new virtual community' that will reinvigorate a sluggish civic citizenry (ibid.: 171).

Despite these three areas of connectedness, people may find it increasingly difficult to belong to communities as a result of these rapid changes, feeling more disconnected and alienated. This is not simply people's sense of 'nostalgia' or a 'false consciousness', but is a trend of diminishing membership in communities and associations that traditionally developed bonds among people. The diminished participation in communities points us to concerns of an increasingly disenfranchised civil society. Putnam's empirical work takes on similar tones to that of Tönnies, heeding the warnings of a waning citizenry and apathetic civic participation.

Similarly, traditional social settings that brought people together in their day-to-day interactions and associations have dissipated. The long-standing corner stores, the local milkman and postman who delivered to your door every day, the local bank and other neighbourhood institutions, have become less prominent (Bauman 2001: 46–7). Many of these traditional social spaces have largely disappeared with the large supermarket chains, shopping malls and automated banking machines. It is unlikely that any long-term relations will be developed under these circumstances, as it is highly unlikely, even when you do talk to a person, that you will meet the same person twice in the high turnover of staff and the anonymity of large superstores. The uncertainty of 'we will meet again' has, Bauman claims, eroded the traditional ways in which people feel a part of their local community.

Increasingly, we find circumstances of the 'absence of community', whereby individuals do not have a connection or daily interaction with those around them (ibid.: 54). The local social infrastructures that helped to bring people together have largely given way to the more economically efficient mega-stores and malls. Institutions are continually deriving new ways to reduce labour costs through increased technology that again reduces human interaction. Finally, some people exacerbate this phenomenon by trying to get away from others, by hiding behind the gated communities that keep 'undesirables' at bay.

Another increasing trend in contemporary society is the phenomenon of 'exterritoriality', whereby the global elite feels increasingly detached from their nation-state. Individuals who are highly mobile have little allegiance to their native country, and have become part of the new 'cosmopolitanism'. Again, this high level of mobility and detachment from a particular local territory heightens the prominence of community-free zones. Such people do not feel the need to have long-term attachments often developed through the long-term associations with people and participation in local affairs. Instead, what has occurred is a rather different occurrence, 'it does not matter *where* [*sic*] we are, what matters is that *we* are there' (ibid.: 56).

The community, Bauman argues, has become generally defunct. In its place, we have an increasing population feeling increasingly displaced due to a lack of belonging. The increasing popularity of daytime television that probes the lives of individuals is as much a result for finding solace in the fact that others feel a similar emptiness. Through common shared feelings of unhappy childhoods, depression, failed marriages and other unhappy events, people hope to come together as loners. It becomes a 'community of non-belonging' (ibid.: 68).

The proliferation of reality television shows seems to reflect such tendencies. Websites, talk shows, soap operas and reality television all chart the latest unfolding events in the controlled settings of the media. The fascinating aspect is the grip that it has on viewers who, in many ways, feel part of those persons' lives. Instead of forming real relations with people in their actual lives, some viewers develop attachments to television characters and personalities.

Other attempts to find community are often found in the one-time events, such as participation at festivals, sporting events and other exhibitions. For instance, people have a sense of affiliation with their fellow sports fans in the stadium, having a shared interest in supporting their local team. We know that such events will occur in the future, but it is unlikely that people will develop sustained relationships. Bauman defines this as an 'aesthetic community' – an event to be experienced on the spot, and consumed (ibid.: 71–2). It is to break up the monotony of our routine life – not to encompass our life, but create a diversion for a brief moment. It does not provide much long-term personal well-being, nor does it necessarily strengthen the attachment of people. It remains superficial and short-lived.

The sense of loss that people feel will not come about through the aesthetic, one-time events. If we hope for a community that would collectively bring about more good, where individually we may be lacking, we need to search for a long-term commitment woven together by our fundamental rights and obligations. These two variables, Bauman suggests, are the ways in which people have shared common aims toward building a community – a ' "fraternal sharing" kind, reaffirming the right of every member to communal insurance against the errors and misadventures which are the risks inseparable from individual life' (ibid.: 72). It is an ethical community that we long for, and should commit to, that will bind individuals together in a just society.

The trouble, however, is that often the aesthetic community and ethical community become blurred and distorted under communitarian discourse. Such a move again creates divisions and divides, building blocks between people through their differences, and creating secure boundaries and blockades (ibid.: 148). Community in this light means adhering to a homogeneous language and culture so as to be a part of that community. Further, it means creating divisions between those who are a part of a community and those who are external to it.

Whether or not such a time existed when people felt a tremendous unity and homogeneity in a community is difficult to ascertain. Such traditional narratives that allude to unity and homogeneity of a community are being swept away due to the reality of increasingly pluralist societies. These social changes give rise to considering what meaningful communities can arise for individuals.

Putnam and Bauman's pessimism about the decay of community may leave individuals deflated about the current situation in civil society. Yet, the call to revive community through our traditional understandings may not be realistic given changing social circumstances. The factors that previously helped to contribute to community are increasingly becoming ineffective and defunct. The 'homogeneous' society is increasingly absent. *Gemeinschaft* communities that Tönnies so readily espoused used to provide the strong bonds of kinship and solidarity. Yet, such communities created a 'cultural segmentalism' that existed through exclusion and differentiation of internal and external membership (Giddens 1994: 126).

Nostalgic notions of community, cultural pessimism and demise of modern society are not entirely accurate (Beck 1999: 21). The perspective of disintegrating community creates a distorted picture of the societal condition, creating false dichotomies between the individual versus society, the local community versus globalization and so forth. Such distinctions are more fluid and blurred than is often acknowledged.

Given the significant changes in modern society, attempts are being made to re-describe civil society and reinterpret these social conditions for potential renewal of social democracy (Giddens 1994, 1998, Beck 1999). If we recognize that social changes are ongoing and evolving, we do not have to assume a 'doom and gloom' scenario. New communities are evolving that may be better suited to the demands of modern society.

Fundamental changes observed in civil society that affect the core foundations can be explained in terms of 'individualization' (Beck 1999: 98). Unlike numerous misunderstandings associated with this term that conjure up notions of atomism, isolation or a revival of the bourgeois individual:

> 'Individualization' means, *first*, the disembedding of industrial-society ways of life and, *second*, the re-embedding of new ones, in which the individuals must produce, stage and cobble together their biographies themselves. (ibid.: 95)

Traditional constructions of the communities that provided some stability for society are now less influential in many cases. Simultaneously though, as these communities dissolve, new ones emerge and transcend former ones. Traditional communities may lose their significance and relevance for the individuals they once served. Such dissolution, however, leads to new creative ways to find meaningful networks for oneself and others. Individualization is not a whimsical folly of individuals choosing to change the social constructions around them. The overall conditions of civil society partly shape and influence the networks of individuals, and individuals respond in kind to the various demands and influences that society has upon them.

To illustrate this point, let us return to the social circumstances of adults, increased workload and its implications for communal activities in civil society. Increasingly common are two-income parents sharing the financial burden to raise children. Participation in the workforce provides increased economic and material benefits to the household. This decision, however, has other implications for other aspects of society. One's participation in the workforce may presuppose one's participation in education. Further, one's access to varied work may presuppose one's flexibility in mobility or the readiness to be mobile. It may also have repercussions in the private sphere including one's family life and leisure time. 'All these are requirements which do not command anything, but call upon the individual kindly to constitute himself or herself *as an individual*, to plan, understand, design and act – or to suffer the consequences which will be considered self-inflicted in case of failure' (ibid.: 97).

Individualization crosses both political and private boundaries. It blurs the distinctions between the institutions of society and the personal aspects of the individual. It is not surprising that membership of trade unions, partisan political parties and nuclear families is declining. These confined, restricted memberships are losing both 'their polarizing and its creative, utopian quality' (ibid.: 98). The fear often espoused is that civil society is becoming depoliticized, fragmented and isolated.

Yet this worry may be misplaced. New and creative forms complement and replace traditional communities. People may still belong to communities, which fulfil a particular aspect of their life. Temporal and fluid communities may emerge that better suit the needs of individuals, and complement the demands of the individual. Individuals, who previously may have not been able to give the level of commitment and thus time to traditional communities, may now find that single-issue groups may better suit their needs, and still be politically engaged and active in civil society. For example, the speed and support for the protest against the Iraq war in March 2003 saw millions of people around the globe come together to voice their concerns through major demonstrations throughout the war. In London alone, knowledge about the protest gained momentum in only the last few weeks with over one million people coming together. On that day, many people may have felt a part of a community, sharing in their aim and feeling a sense of belonging to those who were also committed. The march was indicative of the new communities emerging, quickly assembled and quickly dispersed. For some, members within other local communities would continue with organizing protests and public statements. For others, it would be a brief moment when they came together to show their support and voice their concerns, but it was soon over.

New forms of community are emerging, despite counter-claims that suggest otherwise. Concerns about a loss of community and a disengaged citizenry may actually reveal a transition period toward new, alternative forms of collective participation.

Opportunities for liberal communities

Conceptualizing community in the current social climate has exciting potentials and opportunities. Giddens and Beck believe that the changing social conditions require individuals to be active participants in creating their biographies, shaping their relations with others, in the context of their external social surroundings. Communities that allow individuals to make informed judgements about who they wish to be reinforce the applicability of liberal principles to social circumstances.

Applying liberal principles to people's participation in communities is more in line with contemporary social conditions. It is apparent that the theoretical principles I draw from liberal theory are consonant with contemporary socio-theoretical analysis. The non-ideal social circumstances of society require new ways of considering community that are not taken for granted, but emerge through individual interests and needs. The responsibility rests with the individual, shaping and forming relationships and being active participants in this process: liberals emphasize a similar point, prioritizing individuals' capacity for a conception of the good.

This leads me to a second point. The socio-theoretical analysis reveals that what remains important is the ethos of belonging to a community rather than a particular form or structure of community. Individuals will continue to have social relationships with others. However, the ways in which these relationships are formed may shift with the surrounding circumstances. For example, while people may find that they do not develop sustained relationships with their neighbours by meeting them at their local corner store and postbox – an example that Bauman (2000) uses – other sustained relations may be created in their place. For instance, parents who may walk their children to and from school may create relations with other parents who do the same. The daily school run may be one such social circumstance whereby individuals in similar circumstances will develop relations with others. The flexibility of communities is a direct response to changing social circumstances. Community can have thick or thin conceptions, and short- or long-term relations. Interest groups, cultures or associations may all refer to some notion of community. The common thread between all of them is not a set structure or criteria, but an ethos of common aims and interests.

The third consideration, however, differs in the emphasis it gives to the role of communities in society. Social theorists appear to have an underlying assumption that communities provide goods to individuals and society through enhanced social capital and trust. Liberals, however, do not take this starting position as given. While community may enhance social capital and trust and, in this way, benefit society, this may not necessarily occur. Communities may be divisive and fragmentary, and create greater alienation of those within the community from those outside.

Again, Bethany Baptist Academy exemplifies this point whereby the promotion of their community is to the exclusion of those that fall outside the Christian fundamentalist faith. The Christian fundamentalist community creates walls between itself and the outside world, rather than building trust and developing social networks with people outside its community. To assume that community, in and of itself, will provide greater social capital and trust in society is insufficient.

A necessary condition of increasing social capital through trust and social networks requires liberal principles to regulate accep-table forms of conduct, internal and external to communities. It further requires an acknowledgement that, while communities may provide significant instrumental goods to a well-ordered society, a state cannot rely on community alone to ensure greater substantive equality. Communities, at best, play a complementary role in ensuring greater trust and social capital in society. It is not, however, the panacea for a well-ordered society. Like other important values, such as care, communities require an under-pinning theory of justice to have the desired effects to which sociologists refer.

This raises a final point with regard to the diminished sense of community in liberal societies and its hoped-for rejuvenation among their citizens. With increasing concern about individuals' diminished participation in communities in society, there has been a corresponding re-emphasis on the promotion of community in schools. Promoting community in schools is not necessarily wrong, per se, as I outlined in the previous chapter. However, it would be a mistake to suggest that schools should carry the entire burden in rectifying a societal problem such as diminished community participation. Simply put, 'schools cannot compensate for society' (Bernstein 1970). Schools are but one institution within the basic structure of society, and should share in the responsibility of promoting within a community a capacity for a conception of the good and a capacity for a sense of justice, but need *not* take full responsibility.

I do not suggest that responsibility for a diminished sense of community has fallen solely on schools, but it does appear that much of it has fallen onto educators' shoulders. If, however, societies believe that people's involvement in shared interests and aims provides goods for society, then the state has some responsibility in creating conducive conditions that foster these communal relations. As I mentioned earlier, according to various social trends and patterns, 'the degree of inequality in modern societies shows the extent to which we ignore each other's welfare' (Wilkinson 1996: 143). This should not be surprising: with increased economic and material deprivation, social problems tend to rise in terms of family stress, domestic conflict, social exclusion from the local community and increased crime and drug abuse (ibid.: 164–6). If sociologists seem to agree that social capital and trust are beneficial for society, then they will also have to acknowledge the role that an egalitarian society plays in creating conducive conditions for social cohesion. Participation in communities for social capital is a larger societal issue that is addressed by reducing substantive inequalities among individuals.

Communities, schools and society

In looking at the changing nature of people's participation in communities, we see a number of interesting indicators. First, traditional community memberships are diminishing, while new forms are being created. Second, the structure of communities is changing to suit people's lifestyles. Third, what remains important is people's connection or sense of belonging to others with shared interests and aims.

Similarly, the application of liberal principles is conducive to these contemporary changes in that the emphasis on individuals' capacity to make informed judgements about which communities are worthwhile for them is an increasingly important consideration. Further, if one of the desired goods of community is to increase social capital and trust, liberal theory provides underpinning theoretical principles for the types of communities that will foster these goods. Finally, if social capital and trust are important components in the stability and well-being of a society, social trends and patterns indicate that a more egalitarian society will create conditions conducive toward these goods.

In the penultimate chapter, I consider concerns about the ability to foster community given current educational circumstances.

Notes

1. While it may appear as if *Gesellschaft* exists only in indus-trialized, urban societies and *Gemeinschaft* solely in rural ones, Tönnies notes that the essence of both is found interwoven in all kinds of associations. These concepts are, it must be remembered, ideal types that signify model qualities of essence. The tendency is for them to be bound together (ibid.: 17). For instance, as the town lives on within the city, ele-ments of life in the *Gemeinschaft* persist within the *Gesellschaft*, although lingering and decaying. This is seen most clearly in late eighteenth-, early nineteenth-century English working-class urban neighbourhoods.

CHAPTER 9

Communities in a Changing Educational Environment[1]

Community is identified as a key educational aim in the National Curriculum in England and Wales. The hope is that schools will reflect the larger communities in which they are embedded and, further, that schools will integrate students from diverse backgrounds within a 'school community'. Both aims overlap in their attempts to foster greater student understanding of themselves and of others who come from diverse backgrounds. Given this directive, schools are assigned the task to promote both aspects of community.

A general consensus exists that current education policies promote competition and, given this assumption, are antithetical to values inherent in community. I wish to address three commonly cited concerns that may inhibit schools' ability to promote community: whether lack of time and flexibility in a prescribed curriculum hinders teachers' ability to teach broader aims such as community; whether community is hindered by performance indicators and monitoring mechanisms, reducing collaboration among students and teachers; and whether league tables and choice reforms encourage competition rather than collaboration between schools in attracting and selecting students. In highlighting these concerns, I consider both negative and positive implications that education reforms may have on schools' ability to promote community.

Challenges
Numerous school reforms have been introduced and implemented in the UK since the 1980s, including more standardized practices in schools and assessment policies, greater parental choice and changes in enrolment policies. The 1988 Education Reform

Act prompted a major restructuring of the fundamental structure of education, particularly regarding the implementation of a National Curriculum. A National Curriculum would set core compulsory subject areas, skills and processes to be taught and at various key stages, and various corresponding assessment procedures to evaluate students' acquired knowledge and skills. Parallel educational policies surfaced in the United States, following similar trends. *A Nation at Risk* (US Department of Education 1983) and, more recently, *No Child Left Behind Act* (2001) prioritize 'stronger accountability for results, increased flexibility and local control, expanded options for parents, and an emphasis on teaching methods that have been proven to work' (US Department of Education 2001).

Common reasons cited in favour of increased standardization emphasize equitable distribution of learning outcomes and consistent pedagogical practices. At stake is ensuring that children have access to a full range of opportunities across schools, localities and regions. For instance, students may have decreased mobility to choose schools outside of their locality. Discrepancies in subject emphasis may influence a student's ability to apply to certain universities depending on specific entrance requirements. Students might have to take an additional year at secondary school, or enrol in qualifying courses, to meet the requirements of a particular university. Creating a standardized curriculum mitigates some of these difficulties by enabling all students to be taught common learning objectives.

Meier (2002) contends that many civil rights activists and African-American movements initially sought increased standardized practices as a way of reducing the racial biases found in local schools and jurisdictions. Discrepancies in testing procedures and what constituted a solid knowledge base was often seen as favouring upper and middle-class white families. Standard practices set by larger jurisdictions were aimed at reducing the racial and economic prejudices previously seen in schools prior to the 1960s. That said, the standardization movement has arguably gone further and become demonstrably more intrusive than was perhaps first construed. The justification for raising standards as a way of having a more equitable distribution of learning outcomes and consistent pedagogical practices has arguably done much more than this original intention. The optimism that objective measures in standard tests would reduce racial and economic bias, in many instances, has had the opposite effect.[2]

The second issue raises the concern that, without a standardized curriculum, there is a greater potential for discrepancy in the material that may be taught to students. Several factors may influence the depth of material taught to a student, such as: different emphases on aims of education; teachers' strengths and weaknesses; perceived strengths and weakness of students based on ability, social class, race and gender; and greater emphasis on particular areas of knowledge based on local interests and preferences.

However, the implementation of a centralized curriculum has also arguably increased the level of prescription to which teachers must adhere, particularly in the case of England and Wales with the revised National Curriculum in 2000. The level of prescription raises two concerns: one concern is that a highly prescribed curriculum may limit teachers' ability to teach beyond the specified stated curricular objectives; a second concern is that teachers may find less reason to collaborate when there is a prescribed curriculum in place. Lack of time and inflexibility are two main objections that may hinder the promotion of community in schools. I consider each concern accordingly.

Lack of time and flexibility in a prescribed curriculum

One concern posed by teachers is that a prescribed curriculum reduces the amount of time and flexibility in their pedagogy. The first difficulty teachers may find is that they have little time to devote to areas not specified in the curriculum guide for the particular subject discipline. The second difficulty is that the detail given in the specific learning objectives and outcomes reduces flexibility for deviation or expansion in other areas of interest or relevance.

Given increasing and explicit set objectives, some teachers may find it difficult to teach beyond the stated curricular objectives (Whitty, Rowe and Aggleton 1994). This may result in teachers' reluctance to teach cross-curricular aims given the numerous subject-based objectives they are expected to teach. One teacher states that by teaching broader aims in her lessons, students would be confused by the multiple messages being conveyed, by combining the specific subject objectives and the abstract themes set in the aims of the National Curriculum:

> [You] have to go off at a tangent, dilute the actual message which you're trying to put across by confusing the kids with

the other ... other messages ... you know you're trying to
get the message of the subject across, but you're fuzzing it
with other issues. (Whitty, Rowe and Aggleton 1994: 33)

While the teachers agreed on the importance of promoting cross-
curricular themes, almost all were reluctant to develop them
within their specific subject content. Their resistance was evident
by the invisibility and absence of broader aims in the classroom
(ibid.: 32). With teachers feeling curriculum overload and inno-
vation fatigue, it is not surprising that broader educational aims
may become marginalized while subject matter takes priority.

Second, with emphasis increasingly on performance measures,
teachers feel a 'narrowing of focus in their work' (Gewirtz 2002:
80). The increased need for teachers to produce documentation
indicates heightened forms of monitoring and inspection. A head
of art teacher in England describes this subtle shift in pedagogical
practices with increased performance indicators:

[The 1960s] was a very exciting sort of period and the students were producing very gutsy exciting work ... So I felt
that it was a very meaningful period, and through art we
could reach out, create relationships, and also create the
atmosphere where we could see students grow within our
relationships with them ... [It's a] little bit more artificial
now, it's all judged on paperwork and how well students
perform in examinations – and I'm part of the system I'm
afraid. I haven't stepped out of it ... (ibid.: 82)

With increased pressure to measure and assess each of the particular learning objectives, objectives that are difficult to measure
and assess are often pushed to the periphery. It is difficult to assess
whether students have met the expectations of understanding,
fostering and promoting community.

Teachers feel pressure from various monitoring mechanisms,
which in turn encourages a system of demonstrable performance
indicators. This is summed up by an English teacher who states
that she is 'much more conscious of the clock ticking and
therefore [she is] very, very reluctant to have anything interrupt
that time plan' (ibid.: 81). Two worries are brought up in this
statement: teachers do not have the time to do anything else; and
teachers cannot deviate from a curriculum that is specifically
monitored and assessed. Community, as a learning process, is an

aberration to an outcomes-based model and, as such, may be lost to pedagogies that focus on performance indicators and accountability.

Teachers' frustration with a prescribed curriculum and their perceived inflexibility in pedagogy cannot be dismissed. However, I want to consider this criticism, and suggest other possible outcomes that may result from a centralized and prescribed curriculum. One potential outcome is that teachers conceivably have more time as a result of a set prescribed curriculum. Rather than teachers having to develop a curriculum from scratch, a prescribed curriculum could allow teachers to focus on other aspects of pedagogy such as fostering community. It does not have to follow that a prescribed curriculum leads to less time. It depends how much is being prescribed.

Even if teachers remain sceptical about the ability to foster community, given the number of objectives outlined in a prescribed curriculum, community is a key learning objective found in the PSHE and Citizenship curriculum. How effectively community can be taught within these conditions is debatable, but community remains a central and explicit learning objective. Teachers are required to teach community within the more specific subject disciplines.

Finally, a prescribed curriculum does not prohibit teachers from being flexible. So long as teachers address the main learning objectives, it is permissible for teachers to deviate from the curriculum should they so choose. An aspect of teaching is the judgement they bring to the classroom, building upon their strengths and experiences. These pedagogic practices do not necessarily need to change as a result of a prescribed curriculum. While a prescribed curriculum may reduce the range and extent to which teachers can deviate, teachers' pedagogical practices and emphases are still largely self-determined. For instance, the Anglo-European school is able to develop a holistic community ethos within the current educational climate in England. The state school works within the prescribed curriculum, yet is still able to promote community through the formal taught subjects, and as an interdisciplinary aim throughout the school. The Anglo-European School suggests that flexibility is possible within a prescribed curriculum.

In examining the concerns and alternative consequences, two factors become apparent with regard to a prescribed curriculum and teachers' time and flexibility:

1. the nature of the prescription
2. how the prescribed curriculum is mediated

A prescribed curriculum does not de facto create less time, although it does limit flexibility. For instance, having broad objectives within each of the subjects does not necessarily lead to reduced teachers' time, depending on the degree of prescription. It is the nature of prescription that is important. Objectives that address key points, yet allow for some level of openness, may have less of an effect than objectives that are prescribed to a high level of specificity. Any amount of prescription, however, will have some effect on flexibility. This may not necessarily be negative, as is pointed out by Meier (2002), in terms of providing some common threshold of standards that all students must achieve.

If a prescribed curriculum has the effect of increased assessments and performance indicators, then this may create increased pressures for teachers to spend more time teaching to the specific tasks. Increased forms of mediation, inspections and other forms of interference will have some impact on schools. Greater impact may be felt by those schools that struggle in terms of student achievement, where teachers may feel increased pressure to improve student achievement. Conversely, pressure may have less of an effect on those schools that already attain higher levels of student achievement.

The concern that a prescribed curriculum reduces teachers' time and flexibility is valid in so far as teachers are feeling increased pressure to address numerous learning objectives within prescribed curricula. Yet, the ability to promote community may have varying degrees of effect for teachers and schools, depending on the nature of the prescription and the level of mediation.

Less collaboration among teachers

This leads to a second concern regarding a prescribed curriculum. While teachers are concerned about the lack of time or flexibility to foster community within the prescribed centralized curriculum, less collaboration among teachers may become apparent. Collaboration requires time and effort among staff, and a demanding curricular framework (along with numerous coinciding demands) may overwhelm an already overworked teacher. Further, teachers may see little need for collaboration when each of the objectives is directed towards the individual teacher. The inflexibility of the curriculum may create a situation whereby teachers do not have the time to collaborate, or see the need to collaborate when every detail has been laid out. The potential for isolation among teachers is a concern under a highly prescriptive curriculum which is antithetical to promoting an ethos of community.

Performance measures placed on teachers may have an effect on internal competition and distrust. The misgivings about trying to work together, yet compete in other ways, are indicative of internal market mechanisms that are placed within schools. Teachers may be held accountable to the head of a cluster group, which may be accountable to the senior teacher, who in turn is accountable to the head teacher. Such pervasive lines of accountability affect the internal ethos and camaraderie of staff. This is echoed in the words of a head of department who suggests the internal competitive nature between disciplinary cluster groups:

> The cluster team is kind of all empowering and all kind of encompassing and it doesn't really recognise what's going on in other parts of the school much, or other teachers in other areas are treated with a bit of suspicion. (Gewirtz 2002: 193)

While teamwork is encouraged within various disciplines, the predominance of such monitoring and surveillance techniques may place pressures on teachers to perform (Ball 1998). One potential consequence is that teachers may feel overwhelmed by the set criteria and, similarly, may feel that they must compete with other teachers. The evaluation of their teaching will be set and compared with other teachers and their disciplines. This may reduce the willingness of teachers to collaborate if the performance culture dictates a competitive model.

One might challenge this claim stating that participation in team meetings may create a community ethos. Yet teachers complain of meetings increasingly devoted to administrative and technical tasks, while feeling that there is correspondingly less time to collaborate on substantive educational issues (Hargreaves 1994: 78–90). One may further point to the local management of schools as a way for teachers to become involved in substantive matters of the school, providing increased commitment in shared aims and purposes. Yet, a problem remains that substantive matters – such as curriculum and assessment – remain centralized under the National Curriculum. Increasingly, local decisions are limited to technocratic and managerial aspects, and often amount to mere cost-cutting mechanisms (Whitty, Power and Halpin 1998).

Further, the irony of increased meetings is that they have led, in many teachers' beliefs, to a decrease in informal collegial relations (Hargreaves 1994, 2003). Illustrative of this decrease in informal collegiality is the absence of teachers in a staff room at lunchtime. The staff room has the potential to be a collective shared space, yet it is increasingly becoming quiet as teachers find themselves working on their own, either in their classrooms or separate departments, trying to meet various other demands (Hargreaves 1994). The school is, in many respects, a microcosm of larger society, and is not exempt from decreased levels of social capital as a result of increased workloads and less collaboration (Hirsch 1977, Fukuyama 1995, Putnam 2000).

Hargreaves' work on changing teaching environments notes the pervading sense of suspicion and distrust by various teachers and heads in their reluctance to work as a community.

It should be noted that, while increasing standardization, accountability and market mechanisms may provide challenges to teachers and schools, numerous schools still exhibit strong elements of community. Some schools may be less affected by these educational reforms, in that they may exhibit high student achievement rates, and thus may not need to be as concerned about the micro-management of teachers and test results. In other words, high-achieving schools may create a virtuous circle, and may not be as concerned with standardization and accountability measures, when their school is already oversubscribed and achieving.

Further, it does not necessarily follow that a competitive model creates isolated teaching. For instance, one may consider that an effective strategy to attain higher student achievement is for teachers to work collaboratively in this common endeavour. Mission statements are one way for schools to distinguish themselves from others and, in this way, may develop a sense of community. They may focus on pedagogical practices, curricular emphasis or particular educational values or aims.

While critics suggest that this is yet another market-driven reform measure in a corporate culture catering to upper- and middle-class families that are able to choose,[3] it does suggest some potential for schools to define themselves as part of a particular community. Schools may have to develop strategic plans and work together as a coherent unit, in order to achieve desired results.

Another reform used to increase performance in failing schools in inner boroughs of London is to convert 290 schools into specialist schools (DfES 2003e: 9). The aim is that each school will identify and build upon a specific strength through the shared aims of the school. By identifying a specific strength, schools will build upon their level of performance through that shared aim. So, while some teachers have felt a sense of isolation as a result of increased performance measures, this does not need to be the case. It need not follow that increased performance measures *will* result in a decreased sense of community.

Finally, it might be argued that a prescribed curriculum has little effect on teachers' collaboration. For instance, a teacher who devises her own curriculum may resist collaborating with other teachers who fear greater accountability and monitoring. Not having a prescribed curriculum may allow poor teaching practices to be easily concealed behind the closed doors of classrooms. The issue of trust is obviously at issue here, but a prescribed curriculum may reduce those extenuating circumstances where teachers are negligent, and could previously hide their practices because there was no need for collaboration. A prescribed curriculum may help to reduce those instances by having a shared curriculum in which to compare and role-model good teaching practice.

It is not certain whether a prescribed curriculum will inhibit teachers' collaboration. Similar to the first concern, whether collaboration will be inhibited depends on the nature of pre-scription and the extent to which it is being prescribed. Some feel that a prescribed curriculum makes teacher collaboration irrele-vant. Others may view a prescribed curriculum as a way of encouraging teachers to collaborate as a result of common learning objectives. A more influential factor is the perceived competition among teachers to attain higher student achieve-ments. But, again, whether teachers will have to vie for resources and merits based on student achievement, or whether the school will collaborate together to raise student achievement as a whole, seems to depend upon the school ethos.

Competition among schools and exclusive school communities

The third challenge arises from policies that encourage competi-tion between schools for student enrolment. Two particular policies may change the effect on promoting communities: the publication of league tables, and open enrolment policies. The former creates an environment that encourages competition between schools rather than collaborative practices. The latter encourages competition through per-pupil funding in the open enrolment policy, thus encouraging more exclusive forms of communities in the enrolment policies for oversubscribed schools. I will expand upon each of these claims.

According to the stated general aims of league tables, the ratings of schools are intended to do three things. The first is to provide parents with a partial assessment of how their child's school is performing in comparison with other schools. The second is to provide parents with the school's performance indicators over a number of years to see whether it is improving or declining. The third is to help parents in their choosing of schools for children in primary school or, if they are nearing completion of primary school, to provide information regarding the performance of various secondary schools (DfES 2003c).

These explicit aims suggest that league tables are intended to increase accountability, through competition, between schools. The initial aim of increased competition among schools is intended to make schools more 'sensitive to consumer pre-ferences' and 'increase their efficiency of resource utilisation'; conversely, collaboration is seen as reducing choice by providing little incentive to differentiate among schools (Adnett, Mangan and Davies 2002: 91). The explicit aim of increasing competition among schools, however, is in direct conflict with efforts to collaborate (Hay and Wallace 1993).

The second major trend toward competition is open-enrol-ment policies. Open-enrolment policies allow students to apply to schools that are outside their local catchment area. Funding is attached to the student, and the school's funding in based on enrolment. Schools thus benefit financially in being over-subscribed. Likewise, it is counter-intuitive for schools to assist other schools in a collaborative manner. Schools compete for students and, more importantly, compete for 'desirable' students. Assisting schools to become more successful is in direct conflict with notions of community.

Open-enrolment policies further change the nature of the types of communities in schools. If it is to the economic advantage of schools to attain 'more able' students, then schools have an incentive to alter the student demographics of the school popu-lation. Not only may this affect the demographics of a student population in schools that cater for lower socio-economic groups which may not be able to afford to leave the catchment area, but it has the related problem of reducing the budget share of a particular school if student enrolment falls (Levacic and Hardman 1998). Oversubscribed schools can potentially select students who will better serve the interests of the school. These popular schools will create a virtuous cycle attracting desirable students, who cost less and attain higher student achievement. Although the majority of parents who apply to certain schools are successful in attaining their first choice, the appeals procedure for admissions has more than doubled in the last few years (Gorard, Fitz and Taylor 2002b). Schools can thus be sites of exclusive forms of communities, recruiting students who will provide positional advantage for the school in the ratings, and reject students who are perceived to detract from these goals.

Those students that are easier to teach also tend to be less expensive to teach (Bartlett 1993, Gerwirtz 2002). For instance, students from upper- and middle-income classes tend to be less expensive to teach, than those from lower-income classes, with the proviso that the students do not have any special educational needs. Caucasian girls and South Asian students are perceived to exhibit less behavioural problems than boys or African-Caribbean children. Children who may have potential liabilities, such as learning difficulties or behavioural problems, are deficits for schools. These children may not contribute to better performance indicators, and they may require more of a financial investment than other children. It is a virtuous cycle for successful oversubscribed schools to attract better students, to the direct disadvantage of struggling schools. Open-enrolment policies among schools raise concerns not only about the ability to promote community, but also about implications for equity.

This second repercussion sends a disturbing message for publicly funded schools. Where oversubscribed schools are in the position to select students based on their perceived desirability or educational match, this can potentially change the student demographics of the school that is unrepresentative of the larger public sphere. Levinson (1999) argues that, when state schools are able to select students for cultural, linguistic, religious or economic reasons, these schools will create a more homogeneous student population. This is problematic, according to Levinson, as state schools should be representative of the larger public sphere (ibid.: 110–16). By having more heterogeneous schools, children are able to interact and participate with individuals from diverse backgrounds, fostering greater toleration and mutual respect. Allowing schools to be exclusive through selection policies reduces the potential for children to be in heterogeneous environments. If one of the educational aims of schools is to promote community by easing the child's transition from the local private sphere to the greater community, then it is arguable that schools may need to have school populations that are representative of the greater community.

Yet, mixed reaction for 'school choice' reforms suggest that schools can distinguish themselves from others through distinct values communities or 'niche' markets (Adnett, Mangan and Davies 2002). By developing a school community that offers something unique, the school can potentially 'create a market in which it is the only supplier' (ibid.: 94). In this way, schools differentiate themselves from their rivals, offering something to a specific target group and creating, in effect, a particular community.

Interestingly, despite the qualitative research that has raised these concerns, Gorard, Taylor and Fitz (2002a) argue that quantitative evidence on allowing families to state their preferences for schools has not created an adverse 'spiral of decline' for schools. Their ten-year longitudinal study from 1989 to 1999 found only one school among 30 LEAs where market-choice reforms had a direct negative impact on student enrolment. Where school enrolment fell, this was attributed to a general downward demographic trend in the entire LEA (ibid.: 373). The only factors that seemed to create a downward spiral trend at a particular school were those that were labelled under the 'Special Measures' as failing by Ofsted (ibid.: 374). The label of 'failing' has had more of an effect on struggling schools, rather than the preferences that families may make in choosing a school.

Similarly, within regulated and monitored choice schemes, increased flexibility for schools may create a diversity of programmes that can meet a broader range of needs, interests and curricular emphases to match children's educational needs (Fuller and Elmore 1996, Brighouse 2000a). School choice reforms, regulated by market mechanisms, seem to increase inequities between those that are advantaged and those less so (Gewirtz, Ball and Bowe 1995, Whitty, Power and Halpin 1998). However, if school choice reforms are coupled with theoretical principles and regulatory mechanisms that curtail educational inequities, particular school choice reforms may provide greater flexibility in providing varied educational communities (Brighouse 2000b).

Other schools may feel less strain from competitive market mechanisms in open enrolment. Schools that are located in rural areas may already be, de facto, sites of community. Families who live in rural areas are less likely to choose a school that is farther away, since the distances may be greater than if they lived in an urban centre. The school is already likely to attract students from the local community and, similarly, attract staff members who live in the same community. Rural schools thus create, in one sense, community through shared geographic proximity.

Increased competition among schools may have particular implications for schools in urban areas, and particularly those that are located in inner areas. League tables encourage competition and are not conducive to promoting community. Yet, in other respects, vying for students has meant that some schools have developed a unique community ethos. The consequences of open-enrolment policies is not conclusive, showing mixed results between qualitative and quantitative studies.

Reconciling tensions of educational inequalities between school communities

Of the three concerns posed above, the first two concerns – 1. lack of time and flexibility, and 2. less collaboration – do not conclusively demonstrate a direct correlation between the implementation of these educational reforms and the increased inhibition of community. The third concern – that of the exacerbation of exclusive communities through increased competition and selective student placement – does warrant further consideration. In this final section, I wish to suggest how the principle of fair equality of opportunity may provide evaluative criteria to reduce substantive inequalities between school communities.

As I have noted earlier, autonomy-facilitating educational attempts to secure Rawls' notion of fair equality of opportunity state 'first, they are to be attached to offices and positions open to all under conditions of fair equality of opportunity; and second they are to be to the greatest benefit of the least-advantaged members of society (the difference principle)' (Rawls 2001: 42–3). Although much debate revolves around how this principle should be interpreted and applied, Rawls suggests 'those who are at the same level of talent and ability and have the same willingness to use them, should have the same prospects of success regardless of their initial place in the social system, that is, irrespective of the incomes class into which they were born' (Rawls 1971: 72).

The second condition, that of the difference principle, has significant implications then for how schools may select students, especially those schools that create exclusive communities to the disadvantage of the least well off. Schools are a key social institution that help to provide equitable conditions and opportunities for children; conversely, 'educational inequalities grounded in family circumstances will usually violate fair equality of opportunity' (Brighouse 2000a: 140).

The principle of fair equality of opportunity allows for diversity in an education system, yet it also has the proviso of the difference principle. For instance, school communities that specifically address the challenges of less advantaged students could be endorsed. The London Challenge is one such initiative that targets struggling schools within the five inner areas of London (DfES 2003e). This is a multi-pronged approach that hopes to raise achievement levels for students and raise the quality of education in failing schools, particularly in the inner city areas of Haringey, Hackney, Islington, Lambeth and Southwark. Key strategies emphasize strong community initiatives including: twenty new specialist schools; greater parental and community say in their local community schools; after-school programmes and courses for students and parents; thirty new academies to support struggling schools; and a 'collegiate model' with community links between schools and other institutions. The aim is to develop schools that will be responsive to the needs and interests of parents and local communities. Further, the London Challenge hopes that these schools will provide flexibility for innovative and alternative education programmes that better address students' educational needs in impoverished areas. The London Challenge seems to be one such initiative that uses the ideal of community to empower parents and children who have been let down by schools.

The second requirement of the difference principle could regulate the way schools may select students. First, schools that have a particular community ethos may have to admit a certain percentage of least-advantaged students. At minimum, this could be accomplished by a lottery system that does not take into account student talent or family background. Second, opportunity costs for families to transport their children greater distances to a particular school and to provide childcare are more burdensome for poorer parents than for families who are financially well off.

The costs incurred in sending their children to a school at a greater distance involve spending a more disproportionate amount of their disposable income than that of wealthier parents. To overcome this, another possibility may be to provide assistance such as transport funding and before- and after-school care for those parents that work. Third, providing more per-pupil funding that is appropriate for the cost of teaching a more difficult child may lessen the burden for schools to take such students.

At the moment, it is a disincentive for schools to attract students with special educational needs, since the extra funding is less than the actual costs of teaching those students. Providing adequate funding comparable to the costs of teaching the least advantaged students would help mitigate the current disincentive. These possibilities are but a few ways to reduce the potential for exclusive school communities to select only advantaged students.

Schools might claim that selective policies are essential to creating a particular community ethos. Yet this line of argument should be resisted. A school can differentiate through other means, such as particular subject emphasis, partnerships with other schools or countries and so forth. The concern posed by sociologists regarding the greater exacerbation of educational inequality through school choice and competition is valid; the benefits of having diverse school communities need not compromise educational equality. Regulations that curtail selective admissions policies can help to mitigate this form of educational inequality.

Part of the reason that schools have not seen a 'spiral of decline' between popular and unpopular schools is precisely because LEAs have devised initiatives to combat inequities between schools. Again, Gorard *et al.* (2002a) believe that LEAs have addressed inequities between schools through four key strategies:

1. 'local schools for local children';
2. structural changes to provision;
3. accessibility, and
4. managing the admissions system. (p. 380)

The first strategy concentrates on developing schools that address the local needs of the children in the area. The second addresses the way in which LEAs reorganize school provision, by ensuring that all schools maintain enrolment by allocating caps on schools and reallocating students. Regarding accessibility, some LEAs have created incentives to encourage students to attend their local schools by providing free transportation to their nearest school.

Finally, despite the market trends, LEAs have begun to develop cooperative strategies between schools, by sharing resources, redrawing catchment areas to reallocate the distribution of students or introducing 'relative distance' schemes whereby some pupils receive priority over other pupils to a particular popular school based on their geographic location (ibid.: 380–1).

Deciding how best communities might help to address the least advantaged is difficult, yet the difference principle offers ways to evaluate various 'schemes of cooperation by considering how well off the least advantaged are under each scheme, and then to select the scheme under which the least advantaged are better off than they are under any other scheme' (Rawls 2001: 59–60). Allowing a diversity of school communities does not mean succumbing to greater educational inequities. The difference principle may monitor and regulate those communities that exacerbate educational inequality, without necessarily compromising the concept of diverse school communities in its entirety.

Liberal communities and contemporary school conditions

Recent educational reforms to increase performance and accountability through increased standardization and competitive market mechanisms have had a particular effect on how schools are able to build 'school communities' and develop collaborative links to other schools and the greater community. The fact that teachers find increasing obstacles and challenges in promoting community, whether perceived or real, does influence their capacity to foster it in their classrooms and in the school ethos. The sociological literature indicates a concern that increased standardization and accountability has repercussions on schools' ability to foster community.

Some schools, however, foster community in the light of, and despite, current trends in accountability and competition (Hay and Wallace 1993, Adnett, Mangan and Davies 2002). They provide the seeds that generate new possibilities and new ways of constructing communities, and it is to them that educators may wish to look for guidance and inspiration in developing creative ways to promote community.

Finally, in trying to mitigate the potential educational inequalities through exclusive school communities, the principle of fair equality of opportunity provides an evaluative scheme to protect the interests of the least advantaged children. Using this theoretical principle, we can formulate certain regulations that will reduce educational inequalities in school communities.

Notes

1. This chapter was originally published as an article, 'Communities in a changing education environment', in *British Journal of Educational Studies*, 53 (1), 4–18. Permission has been granted by Blackwell Publishers to reprint this article in this book.
2. For an in-depth discussion of some of the unintended consequences of standardization in education, see Meier 2002.
3. I will address the concern that school communities may exacerbate educational inequalities in the final section of this chapter.

CHAPTER 10

Envisaging Liberal Communities

Maxine Greene, a distinguished philosopher of education, once said that it is important to 'do philosophy', not merely to analyse positions and clarify language, but to consider the substantive differences that could be made in our lives by examining questions in a critical and engaging manner (Ayers and Miller 1998). I have drawn upon liberal and social theory to articulate the issues surrounding community and its promotion in schools. The aim now is to recap how liberal theory can inform the way we promote communities for schooling given current conditions in schools and societies. I conclude with a realistic utopian vision that may create conducive conditions for fostering liberal communities in schools.

Realistic utopias offer a vision of what *could* be, 'a kind of futuristic thinking that is rooted in a sensitive appreciating of the potentialities of the here and now – a form, if you like, of realized optimism or anticipatory consciousness' (Halpin 2003: 60). Unlike disparaging versions of utopia, as being unattainable, delusional or simply impractical – in effect, a 'no place' – a realistic utopia offers a vision that could be realized under favourable conditions. This vision is not intended to be a nostalgic portrayal of an ideal scenario that could never come to fruition, but rather a window of opportunity and possibility. This creative thought process releases the imagination, and offers possibilities that might otherwise remain uncovered and submerged (Greene 1988).

It is important to note, however, that the normative considerations offered here are not attempts to *provide* policy. That, I suggest, is best left to policy analysts. Rather, the proposals that I suggest are tentative in nature, yet exemplifying how the liberal normative principles could assist policy educators in discerning and distinguishing better types of communities for practice in schools.

Liberal communities

This section highlights the ways in which liberal theoretical principles inform our conception of communities for schools. The principles are both conceptual and normative in nature. In doing this, we can see how liberal communities provide an evaluative framework from which to evaluate the permissibility of communities in schools, and foster communities that are conducive and essential for a just society.

1. *Liberals value community.* A meaningful aspect of many people's lives is their sense of belonging and attachment to other people who hold similar views. In ensuring a capacity for a conception of the good, liberals provide rules and regulations to allow for this worthwhile endeavour.
2. *The values of community and liberal justice function at two different and distinct levels.* The basic structure of society is underpinned by the fair terms of social cooperation. Liberal theory identifies reciprocity and mutuality as necessary communal dispositions for the stability of a well-ordered society. In this way, the fair terms of social cooperation realize a distinctive vision of community necessary for the overarching political structure of society. Within this overarching structure, we may see, however, myriad communities, whose influence on individuals' lives may or may not be in keeping with the principles that characterize the inclusive societal community.
3. *Liberal communities may range in structure, form, and scope.* Communities need not be constitutive. The myriad communities within the overarching political structure do not need to adhere to a particular structure to determine whether or not they are communities. The critical point is people's sense of shared belonging and commitments. People may belong to multiple, and even contradictory, communities. They may find a sense of belonging with their culture or race, through associations and networks, or in clubs and interest groups. They may switch communities throughout the course of their life, as free and equal persons. This flexibility is conducive to the changing circumstances found in civil society.
4. *Liberal theory provides an evaluative mechanism for collective practices*

that infringe on individual rights. A liberal conception of community provides an evaluative mechanism for discerning communities that may be detrimental. Not all communities are good, nor are all bad. However, deciding how to make key distinctions between various communities is a thorny process. Liberal theory provides two normative principles for distinguishing worse types of communities that it would be justifiable to constrain in educational contexts.

5. *Communities must observe the constraints of justice.* The principles of liberty and equality provide an evaluative mechanism for communities. If communities are to be allowed, they must follow these two basic principles. Communities must respect and protect individual interests. The principle of liberty aims to ensure that the basic rights of the child are protected. Communities that suppress a child's learning, or cause other injustices that may hamper a child's development and infringe their individual rights, should provide sufficient justification for states to challenge those community practices.

6. *The principle of equality requires that no community benefits to the unfair detriment of disadvantaged persons or communities.* The equality principle states that inequalities can be justified only if they are to the benefit of the least advantaged. School communities that produce further inequalities to the detriment of the least advantaged cannot be justified in liberal theory.

7. *Liberal communities allow for diversity within the boundaries of reasonable pluralism.* Ideally, liberals hope that schools will foster and encourage liberal ideas in school environments. Other communities may be in tension with liberal ideals, but can be accommodated so long as they do not override fundamental rights and protection defined in liberal theory. A range of communities can be permitted in schools so long as school communities do not infringe the development of children as free and equal persons.

8. *Liberal communities reduce educational inequality among school communities through fair equality of opportunity.* The difference principle provides an evaluative mechanism to create conditions to benefit the least advantaged members of society. School communities selecting on the basis of 'suitability' or 'match' would only be able to do so, so long as this did not disadvantage the less privileged children, or those that are more difficult to teach.

9. *Liberal communities in schools will facilitate the development and*

exercise of children's capacity for a conception of the good. Children require opportunities to understand, pursue and revise their conception of the good. Providing a choice of various communal opportunities is a pivotal aspect to developing autonomous persons.

10. *Liberal communities will facilitate the development and exercise of children's capacity for a sense of justice.* Developing communal dispositions of mutual respect and reciprocity underpin a stable and well-ordered society. Understanding these communal dispositions through exposure to and participation in communities is a key aspect to securing children's future opportunities as political persons in a liberal society.

These theoretical principles inform education policy and practice as to the permissibility and promotion of particular communities for schooling.

Future considerations

Given these theoretical principles, what might a good 'community' school look like under ideal circumstances? Many of the hypothetical scenarios and favourable conditions are not necessarily new, or even radical, but have been used in various educational locations in the past and some continue in the present. The final aim is to imagine what elements could be employed in educational contexts to make liberal communities more likely in schools, and what general initiatives one might implement.

A common thread through this book is the need for the physical structure of schools to be more conducive to the fostering of community (Gordon, Holland and Lahelma 2000). As in the visions of many community educators (Neill 1968, Watts 1980, Rée 1985), schools may have informal public spaces for students, staff and parents to meet. Some schools have developed indoor and outdoor courtyards for individuals to meet and chat. Others have developed shared common staff and parent rooms to encourage dialogue and communication. The need for a safe outdoor space also seems to be another factor for allowing children to play before, during and after school hours. The school as a community site is still apparent in pockets of the United Kingdom (Potter 2002b), where the school and community become blurred through integrated and collaborative projects both during and after school hours. Seeing the school as a centre of community that welcomes children and adults alike is one such small ideal that can be put into practice in the space of the school.

Some schools have become creative by putting teachers in close proximity to one another in the same area of a school in order to create a better sense of community within these heavily populated schools (Meier 2002). In these 'open corridors', teachers attempt to collaborate through dialogue and collaboration. The corridor is open to students, staff, parents and the public to participate and view the work that is being done in this part of the school. In effect, the school creates a 'minischool' within the larger school population (ibid: 26). Other schools have adopted this technique, more commonly in the United States, where students are put into specific corridors or cohorts, in attempts to create a better sense of community. These steps taken, albeit small and fragile, show the potential for making small adjustments that may create a better sense of community.

This idea is not revolutionary, but is in stark contrast to some present examples of schools. Due to a heightened sense of fear and perceived need for security, metal scanners have been placed at the entrances to some secondary schools in the United States. Many schools have a strict policy that no strangers, including parents, are allowed on the premises of the schools, only to meet their child at the gated entrance of the school grounds. Similar restrictions are apparent in areas of London and England, with parents waiting outside the gated wall of a school before and after school. Some schools have no green space for children to play, substituting either asphalt or, worse, nothing. Inside, many schools are built with narrow hallways and few open spaces, inhibiting students and staff from meeting or chatting.

The right type of physical environment is but one factor to create a more communal atmosphere. Similar to the physical spaces, creating an environment in which individuals are able to create meaningful relationships is another ideal that is attainable, but requires attention and thought by educators. As has been mentioned throughout, a liberal community school may have a smaller student population which makes it easier to develop trusting relationships between people (Ayers 2000).

Having a smaller ratio of students to adults with fewer staff turnovers may increase the likelihood of children being able to form relationships with fellow students and teachers. Creating professional communities for staff that do not meet merely on technical matters, but regularly meet to discuss substantive issues, may strengthen levels of trust and collaboration. Similarly, and just as importantly, having student involvement and input into school matters, appropriate to the child's age, may help to include children in decisions about their own learning. Participation of parents and external community members is yet another tangible way of bringing the community to the school. Schools that exhibit some or all of these traits seem to foster stronger levels of commitment and ownership among the inhabitants of the school, and often elicit a communal spirit (Apple and Beane 1999).

Pedagogy and a curriculum that are sensitive to the ideals of liberal community may also have subtle, and perhaps radical, implications. If the aim is to promote ideals of liberal community in which the child is central, then reciprocity and mutuality will play a key role. Assessment policies that reflect communal dispositions and allow for variance in how we assess children, not only through individual testing, but including collaborative means of assessment, may alter the competitiveness and rivalry between students. The reduction of league tables and testing, for instance, may have implications for how students explore and experience others, without having to be judged constantly through individual summative evaluations. Providing increasing value to formative means of assessment, for instance, may have different implications for how children learn, which in turn may alter the ways in which children may be willing to share and contribute to other students' learning and development.

Similarly, having particular opportunities in schools, or access to community groups in partnerships with schools for children to join various community clubs may be a key component for children's development and participation. Having support from the community to develop these skills through community programmes may ease the burden under which schools must provide these programmes and also involve the community in meaningful ways. The London Challenge initiative hopes to rejuvenate this possibility, creating federations in which schools can build upon the strengths of other institutions, and create collaborative relationships through these networks and associations.

External recommendations by governments and external community organizations can also assist and build liberal communities in schools. Again, if we are sincere about children thriving in communities, it makes sense for children to have their basic needs met. As I addressed earlier, Wilkinson's study (1996) makes this correlation between healthy individuals and stronger communities. It is unrealistic to assume that we can build healthy communities with children, if their primary needs are not met. Ensuring that children receive adequate care, whether it is through national day cares, or subsidized family support to ensure that children are not neglected or left unattended is yet another safeguard that would help strengthen liberal communities. These policy reforms help to mitigate social and economic disadvantage to particular children, who may not have the same advantages that middle or upper-income families have.

Some may say that the ideals I have envisaged are unrealistic and much too costly to implement. Others may criticize these reforms as nostalgic, or as not necessarily central to promoting communities. Yet, addressing social inequities is an integral aspect of creating liberal communities. Developing a liberal conception of communities in schools requires a commitment from schools and a concomitant responsibility of society. Symbolic forms of community such as uniforms, pep rallies, school teams, may help to rally individuals together in a spirit of community, but structural and policy changes may assist these enthusiastic local gestures leading to more widespread reform and substantive change.

Promoting community need not be an arduous task. The principles that I have put forward are neither cumbersome nor constricting. Only minimal attention is required to the ways in which community might be encouraged in schools and through their local communities that will not produce further educational inequalities nor marginalize certain groups.

Schools of inspiration

While the prescriptive measures that I suggest are deliberately open-ended and broad, there are schools of inspiration to which we can point that exemplify liberal communities in action.

The small-schools movement in the United States is a promising initiative, not necessarily because promoting community is an explicitly desired result, but because it attempts to create environmental conditions that may lend themselves to promoting liberal principles that encourage a particular community that attends to diverse individual needs.

The small-schools movement is one that particularly addresses the issue of school population. The argument starts from the premise that large school populations are more likely to create a student environment that harbours 'disconnection, alienation, hopelessness, and despair' (Ayers 2000: 8). According to Ayers, the most cited reason that students drop out of school is because adults do not care whether they stay in school or not. Teachers cannot provide a level of care and concern for students when the structure inhibits developing close and long-term relationships. The creation of large student populations that house over a thousand students, and sometimes reaching upwards of over five thousand students, is particularly prominent in North America, and becoming more so in other Western industrialized nations. In these circumstances, teachers may teach fifty-minute block periods, to classes of around thirty plus children, teach five classes a day and be in contact with over a hundred and fifty students per day. This does not provide adequate time to develop meaningful relationships with students, or attend to their learning and developmental needs adequately.

Students have difficulty creating relationships with their peers for similar reasons. If students are being shuffled to various classes, and having different fellow students in each class, it becomes increasingly difficult for them to form friendships and bonds. How, then, can schools plausibly create communities of respect and cooperation, when the physical school environment makes this difficult even to attempt?

The small-schools movement is thus an attempt to create preconditions to make schools more conducive to foster communal spirit within a school, primarily by limiting the total student population and by setting conditions by which students have fewer teachers. The hope is that each student will be well known by at least one caring adult, and that students can realistically have the capacity to be a part of a 'community of learners' (ibid.: 5). The point, however, is not to make schools smaller for the sake of them being more 'cosy'; rather, such schools hope to foster social justice by ensuring that each and every pupil is attended to and cared for by a teacher; each pupil is not lost in masses and is more able to create shared ties to others, and that ultimately, each pupil will excel and succeed both personally and academically in such an environment. It is these goals that make the small-schools movement enticing and noteworthy for liberal educators.

While size may make fostering a sense of community in schools more possible, we need to be mindful that a smaller student population will not necessarily create community by itself. Other policies come into play in our creation of communities based on cooperation and respect. Given this caveat, the promise of the small-schools movement offers a potential opportunity to turn around schools that have become unruly in size, and create conducive conditions for promoting community that attends to individual needs.

Integrated schools in Northern Ireland are yet another bold initiative to bring historically fighting Irish Protestant and Catholic communities together under one school roof. In the late 1970s a parent lobby group, All Children Together (ACT), pressed the government to develop 'integrated schools'. The idea simply was to educate both Protestant and Catholic pupils together. This initiative, if accepted, would be a radical change, given that schools were controlled and run separately by the two Churches granted by the Government of Ireland Act in 1920 (Smith 2001: 561). The influence of the Church-controlled school would thus be felt at different levels, most notably, 'parochially organised, denominationally segregated, and clerically managed' (ibid.: 561).

The idea of integrated schools is a large step away from the segregated Church-controlled schools in Northern Ireland. Protestant schools are 'controlled' schools, Protestant run and 100 percent funded by the government. Catholic schools are voluntary maintained schools, run by boards of governors nominated by Catholic trustees along with parents, teachers and board members from the Education and Library Board, and are also 100 percent funded by the government.

Given the historically and politically volatile history of Northern Ireland, the move towards integrated schools was not an easy path to forge. Segregation of the two community groups was sharp. Geographical divides were obvious, as were the distinct segregation between the two groups: simply put, the two would never meet. The political situation of the 1970s and 1980s was particularly violent, and especially in 1981, the time when the first integrated school was scheduled to open. 117 people died that year, culminating in the highly publicized hunger strikes that lead to the deaths of 20 Republican political prisoners to whose fate Margaret Thatcher and the British government were deaf.

Despite this incredibly turbulent time, the strength of the growing ACT parent lobby group successfully acquired its first integrated school in 1981 with 28 pupils in Belfast. A main impetus for the creation of integrated schools was a relatively simple one: many parents had not met a person of the other faith until they reached adulthood. The segregation of Catholics and Protestants was so pervasive that one could literally go through childhood never meeting or talking to the other community. Most parents regretted the lack of this most basic form of social cohesion between communities, and expressed a desire for it not to occur with their own children (O'Connor 2002).

Integrated schools follow a Christian ethos respecting both faiths. Success of the integrated schools is believed to be largely due to the commitment of parental involvement, a respect within the Christian ethos and constitutional and structural safeguards to ensure that both faiths are treated with equal respect (Smith 2001). These basic principles provide a basic, yet successful, framework, achieving some interesting and positive outcomes.

Students in these schools suggest that they do have 'inter-community' friendships: friendships that go beyond their own faith group (McGlynn et al. 2004). This is significant because other schools that may have similar inter-cultural communities may not achieve the same outcomes. For instance, just because a school may have student demographics from various ethnic or racial groups, it is common for these groups to remain segregated within the school walls during non-teaching times. Contrary to this pattern, the research conducted from integrated schools seems to suggest otherwise (McGlynn et al. 2004).

A balance, however, seems to prevail in maintaining pupils' social identity with their ethno-political groups, yet broaden their understanding, tolerance and respect for the other groups. McGlynn, Niems, Cairns and Hewstone's research (2004) indicates that pupils do not have a sense of weakening their own identity, but rather feel that integrated schools helped to strengthen it while becoming more conscious and aware of the other faith's perspective. This stronger sense of one's own social identity and of others' is believed to be attributable to a couple of factors. First, pupils were made to challenge and question their own assumptions about their faith. Second, they were then asked to consider the other faith's perspective, trying to understand their perspective and their traditions. This twofold process, they believe, not only strengthened their own social identity, but they believed created an 'integrated' identity based on broad-mindedness, understanding and tolerance.

The ideals of integrated schools have not been, however, without their challengers. Although it is difficult for opponents to directly attack the aims of the schools (given that they are trying to bring Protestants and Catholics together in an act of understanding and respect), criticisms have come in indirect ways. One of the main challenges is the parent demographics of the students, initially coming from Protestant middle-class families located in Protestant areas. The first school, Lagan College, was set up in South Belfast in an affluent Protestant area. Challengers question whether the ideals of the integrated school would have worked as well had it been located in a working-class district in a Catholic area. While the growth of integrated schools has lessened the strength of this argument, it has not yet disappeared.

Parallel to the middle class is that behind this ideal of integrated schools, it masks middle-class parents who wish to govern a school and mimic a private school setting, using government funds. The active parental involvement and commitment to integrated schools is strong and powerful, which may warrant the altruistic intentions of these parents. Yet, as one head makes clear, had it not been for parents' activism for integrated schools in the first place, then integrated schools would probably not have been created. It is natural, then, to see strong parental interests and involvement in the day-to-day governance of the school given the type of parents it attracts (ibid.: 28–32).

The strongest criticism comes from both established religions. Protestants argue that the whole conception of integrated schools is an artificial one that could easily be created if voluntary maintained Catholic schools were abolished and pupils had to attend state-controlled Protestant schools. A less severe option is the mere fact that many Protestant state-controlled schools already include Catholics.

The Catholic clergy, on the other hand, are concerned about two things in particular: 1. that integrated schools may weaken Catholic pupils' own faith, and 2. that integrated schools do not exhibit a balance between the two faiths, and rather have a Pro-testant ethos, making only token gestures to Catholicism. It is interesting to note that the Catholic clergy have been savvy enough not to suggest that integrated schools are inferior to Catholic schools, but they do play on the guilt of parents who may thus weaken their child's own sense of religious and cultural identity.

Despite the growing pains of integrated schools and some of the daily challenges that integrated schools face, their attempts to bridge the tensions between Catholics and Protestants in North-ern Ireland are commendable. The first aim that becomes apparent in integrated schools is one of reciprocity. Parents who are committed to sending their children to integrated schools believe that it is important for their children (and themselves in the process) to come together from two historically hostile communities, and find some basic shared forms of understanding and while living together peacefully under one roof.

The second is the balance in trying to find a shared political community through its governance of the schools in their regulations, policies and practices, yet trying to balance each individual's community within the umbrella political community. There is no explicit attempt to assimilate or conform one culture to the other, but rather to respect and value each other's communities, within the larger governing structure. This parallels the philosophically abstract notion that I tried to explain in Chapter 5 of the two-part liberal conception of community. Integrated schools, at least in part, exemplify this conception.

I have written a positive report on integrated schools, knowing that one can too easily create an almost 'utopian' image of them. I acknowledge that the balance of the two faiths requires more work, and that the broader implications for how integrated schools will help foster liberal communities in broader society is still in its infancy. Yet the values and principles that underpin integrated schools offer much to illustrate how a liberal conception of community might look in very real circumstances.

Conclusion

Schools continue, as they have done in the past, to foster community. Using liberal theory to assist educators in the types of community that are built around the tenets of social justice ensures that those communities will benefit the child and, in turn, benefit society. Further, using liberal theory as a safeguard provides educators with a way to distinguish between particular communities that may be disadvantageous to some children. Finally, liberal theory provides normative principles for the types of educational and societal policies that would be beneficial for students.

These broad principles, however, lead us to consider communities in particular ways and with particular ramifications. Liberal communities allow for diverse and multiple ways of living and, reciprocally, require that individuals accept and respect differing ways of living. Participating in community develops people's dispositions of how to live together and, to that degree, it is a vital task of educators to create opportunities whereby students can learn to function well and negotiate their participation in communities. Finally, particular communities can contribute toward an individual's autonomy, enabling them to make informed judgements about how they are to lead a life that is worthwhile and meaningful.

Flexibility of structures in liberal communities is also conducive to rapidly changing circumstances in society. Communities need not be constitutive or homogeneous, but may fit under the liberal framework of a 'community of communities'. What some may call communities may not be so for others. Similarly, they may vary in breadth and depth, and time and space. This need not dilute a rich conception of community, for what remains important is that the shared aims and purposes are worthwhile to an individual during the course of her life. Liberal communities allow for individuals to belong to multiple communities, varying in thick or thin conceptions – all of which are permissible within the boundaries of reasonable pluralism.

The flexibility of liberal communities need not result in a meaningless aim for schools in an 'anything goes' manner. The fair terms of social cooperation set out specific cooperative dispositions that are essential to a well-ordered society. Reciprocity and mutuality are dispositions that are to be fostered in schools. Keeping in mind the specific development of these cooperative dispositions, together with that of facilitating children's capacity for a conception of the good, we see the value and need for schools to promote these specific aims.

Liberal communities, therefore, provide a way in which to reduce the problematic aspects of community, allow for myriad communities and foster particular communal aims necessary for a just society. In these ways, a liberal conception of community reconciles many of the ambiguities and tensions that have persisted in community discourse for schools and society.

References

Adnett, N. and Davies, P. (2000), 'Competition and curriculum diversity in local schooling markets: theory and evidence', *Journal of Education Policy*, 15 (2), 157–67.

Adnett, N., Mangan, J. and Davies, P. (2002), 'The diversity and dynamics of competition: evidence from two local schooling markets', *Oxford Review of Education*, 28 (1), 91–117.

Alluli, G. (1990), 'Italy: the *territorio* approach', in C. Poster and A. Kruger (eds), *Community Education in the Western World*. London: Routledge.

Anglo-European School (2003), Anglo-European School website. http://www.angloeuropean.essex.sch.uk/interweb/cosmos.htm. Accessed 15 September 2003.

Apple, M. and Beane, J. (eds) (1999), *Democratic Schools: Lessons from the Chalk Face*. Buckingham: Open University Press.

Archbishops Council of the Church of England (2001), Schools and the Church of England: Church Schools. www.cofe.anglican.org/about/education/schools.html. Accessed 22 May 2003.

Aristotle (1953, 1976), *Nicomachean Ethics*, trans. J. A. K. Thomson, revised with notes and appendices by H. Trendennick; Introduction and Bibliography by J. Barnes. London: Penguin Books.

Aristotle (1962, 1992), *The Politics*, trans. T. A. Sinclair, revised and re-presented by T. J. Saunders. London: Penguin Books.

Armytage, W. H. G. (1961), *Heavens Below: Utopian Experiments in England, 1560–1960*. London: Routledge & Kegan Paul.

Arthur, J. and Bailey, J. (2000), *Schools and Community: The Communitarian Agenda in Education*. London: Falmer Press.

Austin, J. L. (1962), *How To Do Things With Words*. Oxford: Oxford University Press.

Australian National Curriculum Association (2003), National Curriculum Issues Network. www.acsa.edu.au/networks/netpages/national_curriculum.htm. Accessed 12 June 2003.

Ayers, W. (2000), 'Simple justice: thinking about teaching and learning, equity, and the fight for small schools', in W. Ayers, M. Klonsky and G. Lyon (eds), *A Simple Justice: the challenge of small schools*. New York: Teachers College Press.

Ayers, W. and Miller, J. (eds) (1998), *A Light in Dark Times: Maxine Greene and the Unfinished Conversation*. New York: Teachers College Press.

Ball, S. (1998), 'Performativity and fragmentation in "postmodern schooling"', in J. Carter (ed.), *Postmodernity and the Fragmentation of Welfare*. London: Routledge.

Barber, B. (1998), *A Place for Us: How to Make Society Civil and Democracy Strong*. New York: Hill & Wang.

Bartlett, W. (1993), 'Quasi-markets and educational reforms', in J. LeGrand and W. Barlett (eds), *Quasi-markets and Social Policy*. London: Macmillan.

Bauman, Z. (2001), *Community: Seeking Safety in an Insecure World*. Cambridge: Polity Press.

Beck, U. (1999), *The Reinvention of Politics: Rethinking Modernity in the Global Social Order*. Cambridge: Polity Press.

Becker, H. J., Nakagawa, K. and Corwin, R. G. (1995), 'The charter school movement: preliminary findings from the first three states', paper presented at the Annual Meeting of the American Educational Research Association, New Orleans, 18–22 April.

Belenky, M., Clinchy, B., Goldberger, N. and Tarule, J. (1986), *Women's Ways of Knowing: The Development of Self, Voice, and Mind*. New York: Basic Books.

Bell, D. (1993), *Communitarianism and its Critics*. Oxford: Clarendon Press.

Bernstein, B. (1970), 'Education cannot compensate for society', *New Society*, 387, 344–7.

Blackmore, J. (1999), 'Localization/globalization and the midwife state: strategic dilemmas for state feminism in education?' *Journal of Education Policy*, 14 (1), 33–54.

Bourdieu, P. (1986), 'Forms of capital', in J. E. Richardson (ed.), *Handbook of Theory of Research for the Sociology of Education*. London: Greenwood Press.

Bowles, S. and Gintis, H. (2002), 'Social capital and community governance', *The Economic Journal*, 112, 419–36.

Brighouse, H. (2000a), *School Choice and Social Justice*. Oxford: Oxford University Press.

—— (2000b), *Educational Equality and the New Selective Schooling*. London: Philosophy of Education Society of Great Britain.

—— (2002a), 'What rights (if any) do children have?', in D. Archard and C. Macleod (eds), *The Moral and Political Status of Children*. Oxford: Oxford University Press.

—— (2002b), 'Faith-based, schools in the UK: an unenthusiastic defence of a slightly reformed status quo', paper presented at the Faith Based Schools Conference, Institute of Education, University of London, 18–20 June 2002.

Britzman, D. (1991), *Practice Makes Practice: A Critical Study of Learning to Teach*. New York: State University of New York Press.

Burgess, A. (1990), 'Co-education – the disadvantages for schoolgirls', *Gender & Education*, 2 (1), 91–5.

Burtonwood, N. (2003), 'Social cohesion, autonomy and the liberal defence of faith schools', *Journal of Philosophy of Education*, 37 (3), 414–25.

Calderwood, P. (2000), *Learning Community: Finding Common Ground in Difference*. New York: Teachers College Press.

Callan, E. (1997), *Creating Citizens: Political Education and Liberal Democracy*. Oxford: Clarendon Press.

Campbell, J. (1998), 'Dewey's conception of community', in L. Hickman (ed.), *Reading Dewey*. Bloomington: Indiana University Press.

Cerny, P. (1997), 'Paradoxes of the competition state: the dynamics of political globalization', *Government and Opposition*, 32 (2), 251–74.

Church Schools Review Group (2001), *The Way Ahead: The Church of England Schools in the New Millennium*. London: Church House Publishing.

Cibulka, J. and Kritek, W. (eds) (1996), *Coordination among Schools, Families, and Communities: Prospects for Educational Reform*. New York: State University of New York Press.

Cohen, G. (2000), *If You're an Egalitarian, How Come You're So Rich?* Cambridge, MA: Harvard University Press.

Cox, E. (1995), *A Truly Civil Society*. Sydney: ABC Books.

Curren, R. (2001), *Aristotle on the Necessity of Public Education*. Oxford: Rowman & Littlefield.

Daniels, N. (1996), *Justice and Justification: Reflective Equilibrium in Theory and Practice*. Cambridge: Cambridge University Press.

Department for Education and Employment (1997), *Education Action Zones: an introduction*. London: Department for Education and Employment.

—— (1999), *National Curriculum of England*. www.nc.uk.net/home.html. Accessed 20 October 2000.

—— (2000a), 'Raising aspirations in the 21st century'. A speech by the Rt Hon David Blunkett MP, Secretary of State for Education and Employment, 6 January 2000.

—— (2000b), 'Raising standards: opening doors'. www.dfee.gov.uk/opendoor/chap1.htm. Accessed 22 February 2001.

Department for Education and Skills (2003a), Connexions: The best start in life for every young person. www.connexions.gov.uk/partnerships/index.cfm?CategoryID=3. Accessed 13 June 2003.

—— (2003b), Citizenship at Key Stage 4: Unit 07: Taking Part – Planning a Community Event. www.standards.dfes.gov.uk/schemes2/ks4citizenship/cit07/?view=list&column=activity. Accessed 13 June 2003.

—— (2003c), DfES School and College Performance Tests. www.school-league-tables.com/ Accessed 6 May 2003.

— (2003d), Teachernet Professional Development: PSHE home. www.teachernet.gov.uk/pshe/framework/ks4.cfm. Accessed 16 June 2003.

— (2003e), The London Challenge: Transforming London Secondary Schools. www.teachernet.gov.uk/_doc/4170/London%20Challenge.pdf. Accessed 25 June 2003.

Department for Education and Standards (2002), Education Action Zones. www.standards.dfes.gov.uk/eaz/zones_explained/large_zones/. Accessed 22 October 2002.

Dewey, J. (1915, 1977), *The School and Society*. Chicago: University of Chicago Press.

—— (1976), *The middle works, 1899–1924*, Vol. 2: *1902–1903*, ed. Jo Ann Boydston. Carbondale, IL: Southern Illinois University Press.

—— (1916, 1997), *Democracy and Education: an Introduction to the Philosophy of Education*. New York: Free Press.

—— (1984), *John Dewey: The Later Works, 1925–1952*, Vol. 2: *1925–1927*, ed. Jo Ann Boydstom. Carbondale, IL: Southern Illinois University Press.

Dworkin, R. (1977), *Taking Rights Seriously*. Cambridge, MA: Harvard University Press.

—— (1989), 'Liberal community'. *California Law Review*, 77, 479–504.

—— (2002), 'Can there be a general theory of human rights?' Paul Sieghart Human Rights Memorial Lecture Series, British Institute of Human Rights, 18 April 2002, London.

Ellsworth, E. (1989), 'Why doesn't this feel empowering? Working through the repressive myths of critical pedagogy', *Harvard Educational Review*, 59 (3), 297–324.

Etzioni, A. (1993), *The Spirit of Community: The Reinvention of American Society*. New York: Simon & Schuster.

Ezekiel, R. (1996), *The Racist Mind: Portraits of American Neo-Nazis and Klansmen*. New York: Penguin.

Fay, B. (1975), *Social Theory and Political Practice*. London: Allen & Unwin.

Fendler, L. (2001), 'Others and the problem of community', paper presented in Leuven, Belgium, Conference on Philosophy and History of the Discipline of Education: Evaluation and Evolution of the Criteria for Educational Research.

Fletcher, G. (1996), 'The case for tolerance', *Social Philosophy & Policy*, 13 (1), 229–39.

Fraser, E. (1999), *The Problems of Communitarian Politics: Unity and Conflict*. Oxford: Oxford University Press.

Fraser, E. and Lacey, N. (1993), *The Politics of Community: A Feminist Critique of the Liberal-Communitarian Debate*. Toronto: University of Toronto Press.

Fukuyama, F. (1995), *Trust: the social virtues and the creation of prosperity*. London: Penguin.

—— (1999), 'Social capital and civil society', prepared for delivery at the IMF Conference on Second Generation Reforms, George Mason University, 1 October 1999. www.imf.org/external/pubs/ft/seminar/1999/reforms/fukuyama.htm Accessed 25 June 2003.

Fuller, B. and Elmore, F. (eds) (1996), *Who Chooses? Who Loses? Culture, Institutions, and the Unequal Effects of School Choice*. New York: Teachers College Press.

Furman, G. (ed.) (2002), *School as Community: From Promise to Practice*. New York: SUNY.

Gardner, P. W. (1984), *The Lost Elementary Schools of Victorian England*. London: Croom Helm.

Gardner, R., Lawton, D. and Cairns, J. (eds) (2000), *Education for Citizenship 2000*. London: Continuum.

Gereluk, D. (1998), 'Voice, choice and power: contested spaces in charter schools', unpublished thesis, Calgary, AB.

Gereluk, D. (2005), 'Should Muslim headscarves be banned in French Schools?', *Theory and Research in Education* 3(3), 259–71.

Gereluk, D. and Larsen, M. (2002), '(Re)creating school/community relations: the misguided impossibility of returning to a "paradise lost"', paper presented at the Annual Meeting of the American Educational Research Association, New Orleans, Louisiana.

Gewirtz, D. (2002), *The Managerial School: Post-Welfarism and Social Justice in Education*. London: Routledge.

Gewirtz, S., Ball, S. and Bowe, G. (1995), *Markets, Choice and Equity in Education*. Buckingham: Open University Press.

Giddens, A. (1987), *Social Theory and Modern Sociology*. Cambridge: Polity Press.

—— (1994), *Beyond Left and Right: The Future of Radical Politics*. Stanford, CA: Stanford University Press.

—— (1998), *The Third Way: The Renewal of Social Democracy*. Cambridge: Polity Press.

Gillligan, C. (1982), *In a Different Voice*. Cambridge, MA: Harvard University Press.

Gipps, C. and Elwood, J. (1999), 'Review of recent research on the achievement of girls in single-sex schools', *Perspectives on Education Policy*. London: Institute of Education.

Gorard, S., Taylor, C. and Fitz, J. (2002a), 'Does school choice lead to "spirals of decline?"' *Journal of Education Policy*, 17 (3), 367–84.

Gorard, S., Fitz, J. and Taylor, C. (2002b), 'Market frustration? Admission appeals in the UK education market', *Educational Management and Administration*, 30 (3), 243–60.

Gordon, T., Holland, J. and Lahelma, E. (2000), *Making Spaces: Citizenship and Difference in Schools*. London: Macmillan Press.

Greene, M. (1988), *The Dialectic of Freedom*. New York: Teachers College Press.

Gutmann, A. (1987), *Democratic Education*. Princeton, NJ: Princeton University Press.

—— (2002), 'Identity group politics in democracy: the good, the bad, and the ugly', Humanities without Borders Lecture Series, 14 November 2002, Madison, WI.

—— (2003), *Identity in Democracy*. Princeton, NJ: Princeton University Press.

Hall, S. (1991), 'The local and the global: globalization and ethnicity', in A. D. King (ed.), *Culture, Globalization and the World System: contemporary conditions for the representation of identity.* Binghamton, NY: SUNY.

Halpin, D. (1999), 'Sociologising the "third way": the contribution of Anthony Giddens and the significance of his analysis for education'. *Forum*, 41 (2), 53–7.

—— (2003), *Hope and Education: The Role of the Utopian Imagination.* London: Routledge Falmer.

Halstead, J. M. (1986), *The Case for Muslim Voluntary-Aided Schools: Some Philosophical Reflections.* Cambridge: Islamic Academy.

—— (1991), 'Radical feminism, Islam and the single-sex school debate', *Gender and Education*, 3 (3), 263–78.

—— (1993), 'The case for single-sex schools: a Muslim approach', *Muslim Education Quarterly*, 10 (1), 49–69.

—— (1994a), 'Between two cultures? Muslim children in a western liberal society', *Children & Society*, 8 (4), 312–26.

—— (1994b), 'Muslim attitudes to music in schools', *British Journal of Music Education*, 11 (2), 143–56.

Hargreaves, A. (1994), *Changing Teachers, Changing Times: Teachers' Work and Culture in the Postmodern Age.* Toronto: OISE Press.

—— (2003), *Teaching in the Knowledge Society.* Buckingham: Open University Press.

Hargreaves, D. (1996), 'Diversity and choice in school education: a modified libertarian approach', *Oxford Review of Education*, 22 (2), 131–41.

Harker, R. (2000), 'Achievement, gender and the single-sex/coed debate', *British Journal of Sociology*, 21 (2), 203–19.

Harrison, J. (1968), *Utopianism and Education: Robert Owen and the Owenites.* New York: Teachers College Press.

Haw, K. F. (1994), 'Muslim girls' schools – A conflict of interests?', *Gender & Education*, 6 (1), 63–76.

Hay, V. and Wallace, M. (1993), 'Collaboration as a subversive activity: a professional response to externally imposed competition between schools?' *School Organisation*, 13 (2), 101–17.

Held, D. (1995), *Democracy and the Global Order: From the Modern State to Cosmopolitan Governance.* Cambridge: Polity Press.

Higginson, J. H. (1974), 'Dame Schools'. *British Journal of Educational Studies*, 22 (2), 166–81.

Hirsch, E. D. (1988), *Cultural Literacy: what every American needs to know.* New York: Vintage Books.

Hirsch, F. (1977), *Social Limits to Growth.* London: Routledge.

Hobhouse, L. T. (1994), *Liberalism and Other Writings*, ed. J. Meadowcroft. Cambridge: Cambridge University Press.

Hofer v. Hofer [1970] S.C.R. 958.

Jasay, A. de (1995), 'Frogs' legs, shared ends and the rationality of politics', *Journal of Libertarian Studies*, 11 (2), 121–31.

Kasperson, L. B. (2000), 'Anthony Giddens', in A. Anderson and L. B. Kasperson (eds), *Classical and Modern Social Theory*. Oxford: Blackwell.

Kenway, J. (1993), 'Marketing education in the postmodern age'. *Journal of Education Policy*, 8 (2), 105–22.

Kerr, D. (1996), 'Democracy, nurturance, and community', in R. Soder (ed.), *Democracy, Education, and the Schools*. San Francisco: Jossey-Bass.

Knight-Abowitz, K. (2000), *Making Meaning of Community in an American High School: A Feminist-Pragmatist Critique of the Liberal-Communitarian Debate*. Cresskill, NJ: Hampton Press.

Kniss, F. (1997), *Disquiet in the Land: Cultural Conflict in American Mennonite Communities*. New Brunswick, NJ: Rutgers University Press.

Kohlberg, L. (1973), 'The claim to moral adequacy of a highest stage of moral judgment', *Journal of Psychology*, 70, 630–46.

Kohn, A. (1998), 'Only for my kid: how privileged parents undermine school reform'. *Phi Delta Kappan*, 79 (8), 568–77.

Kozol, J. (1991), *Savage Inequalities: Children in America's Schools*. New York: HarperPerennial.

Kymlicka, W. (1989), *Liberalism, Community and Culture*. Oxford: Oxford University Press.

—— (1995), *Multicultural Citizenship: A Liberal Theory of Minority Rights*. Oxford: Oxford University Press.

—— (2002), *Contemporary Political Philosophy: An Introduction*. 2nd ed. Oxford: Oxford University Press.

Levacic, R. and Hardman, J. (1998), 'Competing for resources: the impact of social disadvantage and other factors on English secondary schools' financial performances', *Oxford Review of Education*, 24 (3), 303–28.

Levinson, M. (1999), *The Demands of Liberal Education*. Oxford: Oxford University Press.

Little, A. (2000), *The Politics of Community: Theory and Practice*. Edinburgh: Edinburgh University Press.

Macedo, S. (1995), 'Liberal civic education and religious fundamentalism: the case of God vs. John Rawls', *Ethics*, 105, 468–96.

McGlynn, C., Niems, U., Cairns, E. and Hewstone, M. (2004), 'Moving out of conflict: The contribution of integrated schools in Northern Ireland to identity, attitudes, forgiveness and reconciliation', *Journal of Peace Education*, 1 (2), 147–63.

MacIntyre, A. (1981), *After Virtue: A Study in Moral Theory*. London: Duckworth.

McKnight, J. (1995), *The Careless Society: Community and its Counterfeits*. New York: Basic Books.

Makhaya, G. (2001), 'Young men in soccer take action after personalizing the risk of HIV/AIDS', paper presented at conference on The Politics of Gender and Education, Institute of Education, University of London.

Mandle, J. (1999), 'The reasonable in justice as fairness', *Canadian Journal of Philosophy*, 29 (1), 75–108.

Margalit, A. and Halbertal, M. (1994), 'Liberalism and the right to culture', *Social Research*, 61 (3), 491–510.

Margalit, A. and Raz, J. (1990), 'National self-determination', *The Journal of Philosophy*, 87 (9), 439–61.

Meier, D. (2002), *In Schools We Trust: Creating Communities of Learning in an Era of Testing and Standardization*. Boston: Beacon Press.

Mendus, S. (1989), *Toleration and the Limits of Liberalism*. London: Macmillan.

Merz, C. and Furman, G. (1997), *Community and Schools: Promise and Paradox*. New York: Teachers College Press.

Miller, D. (1989, 1998), *Market, State and Community: Theoretical Foundations of Market Socialism*. Oxford: Clarendon Press.

Mills, C. W. (1959, 1970), *The Sociological Imagination*. Harmondsworth: Penguin Books.

Mohr, N. (2000), 'Small schools are not miniature large schools: potential pitfalls and implications for leadership', in W. Ayers, M. Klonsky and G. Lyon (eds), *A Simple Justice: the challenge of small schools*. New York: Teachers College Press.

Morrell, R. (ed.) (2000), *Changing Masculinities in a Changing Society: Men and Gender in Southern Africa*. Pietermaritzburg: University of Natal Press.

Morris, H. (1926), 'Institutionalism and freedom in education', *New Ideals Quarterly*, ii.

Mouffe, C. (2000), *The Democratic Paradox*. London: Verso.

Mozert v. Hawkins County Board of Education (1987), 827 F.2nd 1058.

Mulholl, S. and Swift, A. (1992), *Liberals and Communitarians*. Oxford: Blackwell.

Neill, A. S. (1968), *Summerhill: A Radical Approach to Child Rearing*. Harmondsworth: Penguin Books.

Noddings, N. (1984), *Caring: a Feminine Approach to Ethics and Moral Education*. Berkeley, CA: University of California Press.

—— (1996), 'On community', *Educational Theory*, 46 (3), 245–67.

—— (1999), 'Care, justice, and equity', in M. Katz, N. Noddings and K. Strike (eds), *Justice and Caring: The Search for Common Ground in Education*. New York: Teachers College Press.

Nozick, R. (1977), *Anarchy, state, and utopia*. Oxford: Blackwell.

Nussbaum, M. (2000), *Women and Human Development: The Capabilities Approach*. Cambridge: Cambridge University Press.

—— (2003), 'The complexity of groups', *Philosophy and Social Criticism*, 29 (1), 57–70.

O'Connor, F. (2002), *A Shared Childhood: The story of the integrated schools in Northern Ireland*. Belfast: Blackstaff Press.

Ofsted (2002a), *Connexions Partnerships: A Framework for Inspection*. London: Office for Standards in Education.

—— (2002b), *Inspecting Citizenship 11–16 with guidance on self-evaluation*. London: Office for Standards in Education.

Okin, S. (1999), *Is Multiculturalism Bad for Women?* ed. Joshua Cohen, Mathew Howard and Martha Nussbaum. Princeton, NJ: Princeton University Press.

Oldfield, A. (1998), 'Citizenship and community: civic republicanism and the modern world', in G. Shafir (ed.), *The Citizenship Debates*. Minneapolis: University of Minneapolis Press.

Peshkin, A. (1986), *God's Choice: The Total World of a Fundamentalist Christian School*. Chicago: University of Chicago Press.

Peters, R. S. (1977), 'John Dewey's philosophy of education', in R. S. Peters (ed.), *John Dewey Reconsidered*. London: Routledge & Kegan Paul.

Phillips, A. (1993), *Democracy and Difference*. Cambridge: Polity Press.

—— (1995), *The Politics of Presence: The Political Representation of Gender, Ethnicity, and Race*. Oxford: Oxford University Press.

Plant, R. (1974), *Community and Ideology: an essay in applied social philosophy*. London: Routledge & Kegan Paul.

Podmore, F. (1923), *Robert Owen: A Biography*. London: George Allen & Unwin.

Potter, J. (2002a), 'The challenge of education for active citizenship', presentation made at the Active Citizens–Active Learning Conference, ETGACE, Brussels, Belgium, 15–17 March 2002.

—— (2002), *Active Citizenship in Schools: a good-practice guide to developing a whole-school policy*. London: Kogan Page.

Power, S. and Whitty, G. (1999), 'New Labour's education policy: first, second or third way?' *Journal of Education Policy*, 14 (5), 535–46.

Pring, R. (1984), *Personal and Social Education in the Curriculum*. London: Hodder & Stoughton.

—— (2000), *Philosophy of Educational Research*. London: Continuum.

Putnam, R. (2000), *Bowling Alone: The Collapse and Revival of American Community*. New York: Simon & Schuster.

Qualifications and Curriculum Authority (2001), *Citizenship: A scheme of work for Key Stage 3. Teacher's Guide*. London: Qualifications and Curriculum Authority.

QCA (2003a), The National Curriculum Online: Music. www.nc.uk.net/nc/contents/Mu-home.htm.
   Accessed 15 September 2003.

—— (2003b), Music Programmes of Study from the National Curriculum, *National Curriculum*. London: Department for Education and Skills.

Rape Crisis (2001), Rape Crisis Statistics. www.rapecrisis.org.za/statistics.htm. Accessed 15 January 2003.

Rawls, J. (1971, 1999), *A Theory of Justice*. Oxford: Oxford University Press.

—— (1985), 'Justice as fairness: political not metaphysical', *Philosophy and Public Affairs*, 14 (3), 223–51.

—— (1993), *Political Liberalism*. New York: Columbia University Press.

—— (1995), 'Political liberalism: reply to Habermas', *Journal of Philosophy*, 92 (3), 132–80.

—— (2001), *Justice as Fairness: A Restatement*, ed. Erin Kelly. London: Belknap Press of Harvard University Press.

Raz, J. (1986), *The Morality of Freedom*. Oxford: Clarendon Press.

Rée, H. (1985), *Educator Extraordinary: The Life and Achievement of Henry Morris*. London: Peter Owen.

Reich, R. (2002a), *Bridging Liberalism and Multiculturalism in American Education*. Chicago: University of Chicago Press.

—— (2002b), 'Yoder, Mozert, and the Autonomy of Children', *Educational Theory*, 52 (4), 445–62.

Ricoeur, P. (1980), 'Narrative time', *Critical Inquiry*, 7, 169–90.

Rogoff, B., Tukanis, C. and Bartlett, L. (eds) (2001), *Learning Together: Children and Adults in a School Community*. Oxford: Oxford University Press.

REFERENCES **199**

Rose, N. (1999), *Powers of Freedom: Reframing Political Thought.* Cambridge: Cambridge University Press.

Rosenblum, N. (1998), *Membership and Morals: the personal uses of pluralism in America.* Princeton, NJ: Princeton University Press.

Rorty, R. (1980), *Philosophy and the Mirror of Nature.* Oxford: Basil Blackwell.

Ryan, A. (1995), *John Dewey and the High Tide of American Liberalism.* New York: W.W. Norton.

Ryle, G. (1949), *The Concept of Mind.* Chicago: The University of Chicago Press.

Sandel, M. (1998), *Liberalism and the Limits of Justice*, 2nd edn. Cambridge: Cambridge University Press.

Saul, J. H. (1997), *Reflections of a Siamese Twin: Canada at the end of the Twentieth Century.* Toronto: Penguin Books.

Searle, C. (1997), *Living community, Living school: Essays on Education in British inner cities.* London: Tufnell Press.

Siraj-Blatchford, J. (1997), *Robert Owen: Schooling the Innocents.* Nottingham: Educational Heretics Press.

Smith, A. (2001), 'Religious segregation and the emergence of integrated schools in Northern Ireland', *Oxford Review of Education*, 27, (4), 559–75.

Stewart, W. A. C. (1972), *Progressives and Radicals in English Education, 1750–1970.* London: Macmillan, p. 71.

Strike, K. (1999), 'Justice, caring, and universality: in defense of moral pluralism', in M. Katz, N. Noddings and K. Strike (eds), *Justice and Caring: The Search for Common Ground in Education.* New York: Teachers College Press.

—— (2002), 'Philosophical perspectives on the school as a community', paper presented at the Philosophy of Education Society of Great Britain, Cambridge Branch meeting, 22 November 2002.

—— (2003) 'Toward a liberal conception of school communities: community and the autonomy argument', *Theory and Research in Education*, 1 (2), 171–244.

Swift, A. (2001), *Political Philosophy: A Beginner's Guide for Students and Politicians.* Cambridge: Polity Press.

—— (2003), *How not to be a Hypocrite: School Choice for the Morally Perplexed Parent.* London: Routledge.

Tam, H. (1998), *Communitarianism: A New Agenda for Politics and Citizenship.* London: Macmillan Press.

Tarule, J. (1996), 'Voices in dialogue: collaborative ways of knowing', in N. Goldberger, J. Tarule, B. Clinchy and M.

Belenky (eds), *Knowledge, Difference and Power: Essays Inspired by Women's Ways of Knowing*. New York: Basic Books.

Taylor, C. (1985), *Philosophy and the Human Sciences: Philosophical Papers 2*. Cambridge: Cambridge University Press.

—— (1992), 'The politics of recognition', in Amy Gutmann (ed.), *Multiculturalism and 'The Politics of Recognition'*. Princeton, NJ: Princeton University Press.

—— (1993), 'The dangers of soft despotism', *The Responsive Community*, 3 (4), 21–31.

—— (1995a), 'Liberal-communitarian debate', *Philosophical Arguments*. London: Harvard University Press.

—— (1995b), 'Liberal politics and the public sphere', *Philosophical Arguments*. London: Harvard University Press.

Temmerman, N. (1991), 'The philosophical foundations of music education: the case of primary music education in Australia', *British Journal of Music Education*, 8 (2), 149–59.

Tocqueville, A. de (1956), *Democracy in America*, ed. Richard Heffner. New York: The New American Library.

Tönnies, F. (1957), *Community and Society*, ed. and trans. Charles Loomis. East Lansing: Michigan State University Press.

Tropp, A. (1957), *The School Teachers: the Growth of the Teaching Profession in England and Wales from 1800 to the Present Day*. London: William Heinemann.

UNESCO (1998), *What Education For What Citizenship?* International project of UNESCO www3.itu.int:8002/ibe-citied/the_project.html. Accessed 5 January 2001.

Unterhalter, E. (2003), 'The capabilities approach and gendered education: an examination of South African complexities', *Theory and Research in Education*, 1 (1), 7–22.

US Department of Education (1983), *A Nation at Risk*. www.Ed.gov/pubs/NatAtRisk/risk.html. Accessed 1 June 2003.

US Department of Education (2001), No Child Left Behind Act of 2001. www.nclb.gov. Accessed 12 June 2003.

Walzer, M. (1983), *Spheres of Justice: A Defense of Pluralism and Equality*. Oxford: Basic Books.

Walzer, M. (1998), 'The civil society argument', in G. Shafir (ed.), *The Citizenship Debates*. Minneapolis: University of Minnesota Press.

Watts, J. (1980), *Towards an Open School*. New York: Longman.

Western and Northern Canadian Protocol (2000), Foundation Document for the Development of the Common Curriculum

Framework for Social Studies Kindergarten to Grade 12. www.wcp.ca/. Accessed 12 June 2003.

White, J. and White, P. (2001), 'An analytic perspective on education and children's rights', in F. Heyting, D. Lenzen and J. White (eds), *Methods in Philosophy of Education*. London: Routledge.

Whitty, G. (1997a), 'School autonomy and parental choice: consumer rights versus citizen rights in education policy in Britain', in D. Bridges (ed.), *Education, Autonomy and Democratic Citizenship: Philosophy in a Changing World*. London: Routledge.

—— (1997b), 'Social theory and education policy: the legacy of Karl Mannheim', extended version of a lecture delivered at the Institute of Education, University of London on 9 January 1997, Institute of Education.

Whitty, G., Power, S. and Halpin, D. (1998), *Devolution and Choice in Education: The School, the State and the Market*. Buckingham: Open University Press.

Whitty, G., Rowe, G. and Aggleton, P. (1994), 'Discourses in cross-curricular contexts: limits to empowerment', *International Studies in Sociology of Education*, 4 (1), 25–42.

Wilkinson, B. (2002), Christian schooling in public schools. www.fotf.ca/if/03-04.02/articles/2.html. Accessed 22 May 2003.

Wilkinson, R. (1996), *Unhealthy Societies: The Afflictions of Inequality*. London: Routledge.

Williams, R. (1979), *Keywords: A Vocabulary of Culture and Society*. New York: Oxford University Press.

—— (1983), *Keywords: A Vocabulary of Culture and Society*. London: Fontana Paperbacks.

Wilson, J. and Janoski, T. (1995), 'The contribution of religion to volunteer work', *Sociology of Religion*, 56, 137–52.

Wilson, J. and Musick, M. (1997), 'Who cares? Toward an integrated theory of volunteer work', *American Sociological Review*, 62, 694–713.

—— (1999), 'Attachment to volunteering', *Sociological Forum*, 14, 243–72.

Wisconsin v. Yoder (1972) 406 U.S. 205 (U.S.S.C.).

Wringe, C. (1994), 'Markets, values and education', in D. Bridges and H. McLaughlin (eds), *Education and the Market Place*. London: Falmer Press.

Young, I. M. (2000), *Inclusion and Democracy*. Oxford: Oxford University Press.

Index